A Caricature H
Canadian P

Events from the union of 1841, as illustrated by cartoons from "Grip", and various other sources

J. W. Bengough

Alpha Editions

This edition published in 2024

ISBN : 9789364739641

Design and Setting By
Alpha Editions
www.alphaedis.com
Email - info@alphaedis.com

As per information held with us this book is in Public Domain.
This book is a reproduction of an important historical work. Alpha Editions uses the best technology to reproduce historical work in the same manner it was first published to preserve its original nature. Any marks or number seen are left intentionally to preserve its true form.

PREFACE.

A "caricature history" does not mean that history is caricatured. On the contrary, a good caricature enables us to see, in a true light, facts that might otherwise be hidden or misrepresented. We understand current events and the social life of England from the illustrations of *Punch* more truly than from the columns of the *Times* or the *Morning Post*. Canada is only beginning life, and our politics touch subjects of general interest so seldom, that it is sometimes thought and said that there is no field for a Canadian *Punch*; but the fact, perhaps not generally known, that for the last forty years, at any rate, we have rarely been without artists whose pictures on the questions of the day have appealed successfully to popular humor, proves that our political life has been robust from the beginning. Some of these artists had to content themselves with publishing fly-sheets that provoked the laughter of the town, but that had no chance of obtaining more than a local reputation. For others, organs well-known in their day, such as *Punch in Canada*, *Diogenes*, and *Grinchuckle*, were established at different times prior to 1873, when GRIP vaulted into the seat which he has occupied since to the satisfaction of all Canada. Requests have been frequently made for a work containing a continuous series of his cartoons, and in now acceding to these it has been thought well to give illustrations of what was done among us in the same line previously. Fortunately the publishers were able to obtain selections from the sources to which I have referred, and also from the *Canadian Illustrated News*; and the First Volume of this work thus gives something like a continuous pictorial history of the events that have stirred popular feeling most deeply since 1848. They believe that those older representations will be heartily welcomed, and they desire to thank all who have assisted in making the work so extended.

As to GRIP himself, he needs no letters of commendation, but, with his well-known regard to the established usages of society, he thinks that there should be a Preface to the work. Considering how freely he takes a hand in our concerns, and that, in order to show us what goes on behind the scenes, he has no hesitation in entering bar-rooms, Government Houses, Palaces, and the Privy-Council Chambers of our pastors and masters, this modesty on his part will be duly appreciated by a modesty-loving public.

A young member of our House of Commons waxed eloquent in the course of his maiden speech, and, naturally enough, some of his brethren thought him mad. Not so thought Joseph Howe, to whom Shakespeare was dearer than all the Blue-books in the Parliamentary Library: "Thank God for a bit of poetry in this dry-as-dust House," whispered the old man to a near neighbor. Yes, and thank God for Humor, with its intuitive perception of truth, and its consequent impartiality. Without GRIP, what Saharas our Parliaments would be!

Every man should take an intelligent interest in the political life of his country. But from what quarter is he to get information? He cannot get Hansard; and even if he could, life is too short to read the terrible volumes. To trust himself to this or that party paper will insure interest but not intelligence; and to read the papers on both sides will land him in hopeless scepticism, or drown him "in a popular torrent of lies upon lies." On the whole, he cannot do better than trust GRIP, as the most honest interpreter of current events we happen to have. GRIP, too, not only generally hits the nail on the head, but sometimes hits like a blacksmith—and we belong to a race that loves to see a blow well struck. Besides, the fellow has no malice in him. He has always a merry heart, and that doeth good like a medicine. Many a laugh he has given us, and laughter clears away unwholesome fogs from the spirit. Along with music it is next best to Holy Writ, according to the testimony of Martin Luther. A picture, too, has this unspeakable advantage over verbiage, that you can take in the situation at a glance, and if it is not agreeable, you can pass on. You condemn the representation as unfair, but, at any rate, your time is not lost.

I do not speak as an artist of the cartoons or the caricatures that illustrate our political history since 1873. To me their artistic merit is exceptionally great, but I am not qualified to speak as a critic of technique. I speak only as a public teacher who knows that the educational influence of pen or pencil may be greater than that of the living voice, and who rejoices when that influence is on the right side.

In this case it is on the right side. GRIP is impartial, in a country where it is very hard to be impartial, and harder still to have your impartiality acknowledged. GRIP is also always patriotic. He is something even better—he is healthy. You may think him at times Utopian. You may not agree with the means he proposes, but you must always sympathize with the end he has in view. He is scrupulously clean. He never sneers. In the best sense of the word, he is religious.

One word more: GRIP'S humor is his own. It has a flavor of the soil. It is neither English nor American. It is Canadian.

Ladies and Gentlemen, I have the honor formally to introduce to you my esteemed friend, Mr. GRIP. You may receive him with confidence into your homes and hearts.

G. M. Grant

UNIVERSITY OF QUEEN'S COLLEGE,

KINGSTON, *March, 1886.*

SKETCH OF
Canadian Political History,

1841 TO 1879

From the date of the English conquest of Quebec and the Treaty of Paris (1763) down to the year at which the present brief historical sketch opens, (1841), the history of Canada is a story of unrest and agitation. The old-world simplicity and pious contentment of the French *habitant* was intruded upon by the advent of the more enterprising Briton, and ere long the inevitable struggle began. The French Canadian, whose language, laws and religion had been specially reserved to him by the Treaty, was not unnaturally apprehensive of the consequences of English domination, and with a new-born energy he awoke to the defence of his rights. His English fellow-colonist having discovered that the governmental arrangements were too primitive and narrow for the comfort of one who had formerly lived under the British constitution, lost no time in commencing the agitation for reform. In some of his views—outside of the sacred reservation referred to—his French neighbor joined him. Hand in hand they protested against the infringement of their common rights by the Governor and his Council, and demanded changes in the constitution. Meantime the English element was growing in the country west of Montreal, by emigration from the old land, and accessions of Loyalists from the newly-established Republic of the United States. The superiority of the British settler soon made itself manifest in the material conquests which he achieved over the forests. The new English Province rapidly surpassed the old French one in prosperity, and the flames of jealousy were rekindled. Ultimate ruin of the colony from internecine strife seemed inevitable unless some adequate remedy could be found. The separation of the rival races naturally suggested itself as that remedy, and as they were already practically divided geographically—the number of English settlers in the French Province being comparatively small—great hopes were built upon a similar division politically. The Imperial Government accordingly in 1791 passed the Constitutional Act, by which the country was divided into the two Provinces of Upper and Lower Canada, each being granted a representative form of government and a constitution supposed to be suited to its population. The governmental machinery provided for each Province under this Act was a Governor, appointed by the Crown, and responsible to the Imperial authorities alone; a Legislative Council, appointed for life by the Governor, and a Legislative Assembly, elected by the people on a suffrage almost universal. The executive functions of the supposedly popular branch of this governmental system were nominally vested in a committee known as the Executive Council, the members of which were selected by the Governor, usually from the judiciary, the membership of the Legislative Council, and the ranks of salaried officials. Practically the Governor himself was the real executive, as his Council thus chosen (and responsible only to himself as representative of the Crown) was regarded by him merely as an advisory committee in grave matters of policy, but as possessing no control over appointments to office, and the various other matters, which under our present system appertain to the executive. This proved a fatal weakness. In both Provinces the Executive Councils gradually drifted away from the sympathy of the people as represented in the Assemblies. The breach became wider and wider, until at length the discontent of the people terminated in open rebellion (1838).

At this juncture the Imperial Government appointed Lord Durham to proceed to Canada and report upon the state and requirements of the country, civil and military. After five months spent in investigation, Lord Durham prepared his celebrated Report, which was duly submitted to the government of Lord John Russell (1839). In this document a legislative union of the Provinces was recommended, and the Home Government proceeded without delay to carry the recommendation into effect. It was thought desirable, however, to secure the assent of the people of the Provinces before passing the Union measure, and for this purpose Mr. Charles Poulett Thompson (afterwards Lord Sydenham), was despatched to Canada. On his arrival (17th October, 1839) he found Lower Canada without an Assembly—that body having been superseded by a Select Council appointed by Lord Durham's successor in the governorship—Sir John Colborne. This Council being chiefly composed of adherents of the British party readily gave the required assent, and subsequently the Upper Canada Assembly and Legislative Council acquiesced. A draft Union Act was forthwith prepared and forwarded to England, and a measure founded upon it was at once passed.

By this Act, the country was renamed the Province of Canada, and the governmental machinery provided was, a Governor, representing the Crown, a Legislative Council of 24, to be appointed for life, and an assembly of 84 members, to be elected by the people, and executing its business through a Responsible Government. This Act went into effect in the year 1841, when the first United Parliament met at Kingston, which had been chosen as the Capital by the Governor. The first session passed off in a manner which on the whole promised well for the new system, although it was made manifest that the people of Quebec regarded the Union as a scheme to which they had not assented—the Special Council, which had acted for them in the matter, having been in no sense a truly representative body. The session was chiefly remarkable, however, for a distinct pledge given by the Ministry—

though with apparent reluctance—that the Government would fully acknowledge its responsibility to the people as that term was understood under the British constitution. This was regarded as a signal victory by the advocates of the responsible system, as the first Cabinet was composed of mixed elements—some of its leading members having been known as pronounced opponents of "Responsibility." The fact that there was no French representative in the Ministry augmented the discontent of Lower Canada, but the election of one of their trusted compatriots to the speakership did something to mollify this feeling.

(From *Punch in Canada*, after the attack by the mob on Lord Elgin, 1849.)

The Governor-General, who, for his services in connection with the Union, had been raised to the Peerage, under the title of Lord Sydenham, was in delicate health at the time of the first session of the House, and died before the second session began, his end being hastened by an accident which befel him while taking his customary horseback exercise. It was some months before the Home Government appointed a successor to the vice-royalty, and during the interregnum the affairs of the Province were administered by Lieut.-General Sir Richard Jackson, commander of the forces in Canada. Meantime, Sir Robert Peel had succeeded to power in England, and, as a natural consequence, the new Governor-General was selected from the Conservative ranks. The choice fell upon Rt. Hon. Sir Charles Bagot, who was known in Imperial politics as a "High Tory," and was a man of acknowledged ability and wide diplomatic experience. The friends of Responsible Government in Canada were apprehensive of bad consequences to the newly inaugurated system as a result of this appointment, but their fears were in due time dispelled, as Sir Charles proved a thoroughly constitutional Governor. Indeed, so conscientiously did he keep within the exact limits of his powers throughout his term of office, that his only enemies were amongst the reactionary section of the Canadian Tory party. The new Governor, when he met Parliament in 1842, found the Sydenham Government still in office, though manifestly weak in the House, and almost certain of defeat on the first opportunity offered. A Kingston paper of the day described this Cabinet as follows: "Instead of being a coalition of moderate men it is a coalition of fierce extremes. How they can meet at the Council Board and not laugh in each other's faces if in merry mood, or come to fisticuffs if in angry one, must be an eighth wonder of the world." In Parliament they were earnestly opposed on the one hand by the old-line Conservatives, under the leadership of Sir Allan Macnab and Mr. John S. Cartwright, member for Lennox and Addington, and on the other hand by the Upper Canada Reformers and Radicals, under Hon. Robt. Baldwin, in alliance with the French Canadian members, who acknowledged Louis Hypolite Lafontaine as their leader. This distinguished gentleman now entered the Union Parliament for the first time, sitting for the fourth riding of York, for which constituency he had been elected on the personal introduction of Mr. Baldwin. A motion of no confidence was moved early in the session, but, instead of allowing the vote to be taken, the Cabinet resolved upon a reconstruction, and after considerable difficulty this was effected by the retirement of three of the Conservative members, and the accession in their stead of Mr. Baldwin, Mr. Lafontaine and Mr. Morin, the two latter being the first French representatives admitted to seats in the Cabinet. With the second session ended the career of the second Governor-General. Sir Charles Bagot was through illness obliged to relinquish the post. His successor was Sir Charles T. Metcalf, late of India and Jamaica, who assumed office in Canada, March 30th, 1843. Sir Charles Bagot died on the 19th of May following, at Kingston. The new Governor-General entered upon his duties with a high reputation for ability, rectitude and independence of mind, and a record which marked him as a Liberal statesman. His eastern experiences and training, however, were against the probability of his success in his new sphere, for a colonial application of Responsible Government was one of those things he did not understand. The Cabinet that saluted him on his arrival is known in our history as the Lafontaine-Baldwin Ministry, and on the assembling of the third session, it was found that this reconstructed Government commanded a large majority in the House. The weakness of the Opposition, composed as it was, in Sir Chas. Metcalf's opinion, of representatives of "the only party in the country upon whom the mother country might confidently rely in the hour of need," evoked the sympathy of the new Governor, and it was not long before the cordiality between him and some of the members of the administration began to wane. It became apparent that the Governor was not disposed to interpret "Responsible

Government" to mean that the Governor-General was a mere figure-head. He claimed the right to exercise a certain amount of patronage on his own account, and asserted that his responsibility in various matters was to the Imperial authorities directly and not to the people of Canada through his ministers. Sir Charles' ardent wish was to obliterate the strong party lines and allay the rancorous hostilities around him, and it is evident that he thought to effect these good ends by appointing Conservatives to various offices as opportunity might offer. In the meantime, while outwardly at peace with his ministers, the Governor openly cultivated very friendly relations with prominent members of the Opposition party.

The session of 1843 began on the 28th of September, and was signalized by a long and hot debate on the subject of the removal of the seat of Government, the ministry having decided to establish the capital at Montreal. The vote finally taken showed a good majority in favor of the removal, though as one consequence of it, Mr. Jameson, Speaker of the Legislative Council, resigned his seat. This resignation assumed some importance as a factor in the developments of the near future, when it came to the knowledge of the ministry that the vacant chair had been offered by the Governor-General—acting, of course, without their advice—to a prominent Conservative, Mr. L. P. Sherwood, and subsequently to another opponent of the Government, Mr. Neilson, of Quebec. Prior to this discovery, however, His Excellency appointed one Mr. Francis Powell (also a Conservative) to the position of Clerk of the Peace for Dalhousie District—of which action he subsequently informed his ministers in a note. This little missive was the signal for a long and stubborn contest, in which the very principles of Responsible Government were considered by the Reform Party to be at stake.

The Cabinet at once deputed Messrs. Lafontaine and Baldwin to wait upon the Governor-General, and to represent to him that in their view the exercise of the prerogatives of the Crown without reference to the responsible ministry was contrary to the letter and spirit of the resolutions of 1841, in which Responsible Government in its fullest sense had been affirmed as the new Canadian constitution. That the Governor possessed certain prerogatives of appointment to office, etc., they did not deny, but they insisted that before exercising any of these the system required him to consult his advisers, who, if they could not approve, had the alternative of resigning. Sir Charles Metcalfe could not be brought to take this view of his duty; on the contrary, he regarded it as derogatory to the dignity of the Crown to accept such a condition, which, he contended, was not contained in the Resolutions of 1841, as he interpreted them. In this position, which he maintained throughout the contest, the Governor appears to have been upheld by Lord Stanley, the Colonial Secretary in the Home Government.

The conference having been without result—except to make the attitude of the Governor perfectly clear—all the members of the Government, excepting Mr. Dominic Daly, Provincial Secretary for Lower Canada, resigned their portfolios. A prolonged debate ensued in the House, which was brought to a close by the passage of the following resolution by a vote of 64 to 23: Moved by Mr. Price, seconded by Mr. Benjamin Holmes, "That an humble address be presented to His Excellency, humbly representing to His Excellency the deep regret felt by this House at the retirement of certain members of the Provincial Administration on the question of the right to be consulted on what the House unhesitatingly avow to be the prerogative of the Crown, appointments to office; and further to assure His Excellency that the advocacy of this principle entitles them to the confidence of this House, being in strict accordance with the principles embraced in the resolution adopted by this House on the 3rd of September, 1841." Parliament rose on December 9th, and the country was thus left without any regular Ministry, in which condition it practically remained for some nine months. In the meantime, Mr. D. B. Viger, a prominent French Canadian, and Mr. Draper (afterwards Chief Justice) had been prevailed upon to join Mr. Daly—and for the greater portion of the period mentioned this semblance of a Cabinet were the only advisers of the Governor. These months, as may easily be supposed, were filled up with vociferous debate on the platform and through the press. The Conservative Party very generally sided with the Governor, and he was not without many able defenders of the course he had taken; on the other hand he was violently denounced and even defamed by the Liberals, who looked upon him and his sympathisers as the deliberate enemies of popular rights. It was during this "interregnum," *i.e.*, on the 5th of March, 1844, that the Toronto *Globe* made its first appearance as an organ of the Liberal Party under the editorship of Mr. Peter Brown and his subsequently famous son, George, and it was the struggle then going on which paved the way for the public career of the younger man. Mr. Viger exerted his utmost influence to win the Lower Canadians to the Governor's side, but in this he signally failed, and when at length after vast trouble the vacant Cabinet places had been filled up, it was so evident that they could command no following in the House that a dissolution and general election were decided upon. The result of this contest—which was bitter beyond precedent—was a small majority for the Government in the Parliament of 1844. Amongst the newly-elected members was Mr. (now Sir) John A. Macdonald, who was returned as Member for Kingston. Mr. Draper resigned his seat in the Legislative Council to assume the leadership of the Government, and it required all his acknowledged ability to weather the storm of the Session, for meantime the Lafontaine-Baldwin Party was steadily gaining strength. While matters were in this precarious condition, the Governor-General was obliged on account of ill health to resign his office, and return to England. Ere leaving Canada he was raised to the Peerage with the title Baron Metcalfe of Fern Hill, but he had worn his new honors but a few months before death relieved him of his sufferings (5th September, 1846). Whatever may be thought of Lord Metcalfe's political views or actions, all who are authorized to speak of him personally agree in describing him as a most generous, kindly and lovable man. Earl Cathcart, Commander-in-Chief of the Forces in Canada, succeeded to the Governor-Generalship after a brief period as Administrator, and under his rule the struggle between the parties continued.

"FRENCH DOMINATION."

(*From Punch in Canada.*)

But that time was fortunately very brief. In justice to Lord Cathcart it must be said that he took no active part in the Government, his attention being wholly occupied by military matters in view of the strained relations of England and the United States over the Oregon Boundary matter. It was chiefly as a military expert that he had been placed at the head of affairs, and the probability of war having disappeared by the ratification of the Oregon Treaty, the Imperial Government relieved him of the Viceroyalty, and selected Lord Elgin, a trained statesman, as his successor. This nobleman bore an exceptionally high character and his official career had hitherto been very successful. Like Lord Metcalfe he left the Governorship of Jamaica to assume that of Canada. In politics he was a Conservative, but could not fairly be described as a Tory in the fullest meaning of that term. The new Governor-General was sworn into office on January 30th, 1847, and one of his first utterances in reply to the usual addresses of welcome was, "I am sensible that I shall best maintain the prerogative of the Crown, and most effectually carry out the instructions with which Her Majesty has honored me, by manifesting a due regard for the wishes and feelings of the people and by seeking the advice and assistance of those who enjoy their confidence." Lord Elgin met his first Parliament on June 2nd. The Government had meanwhile been reconstructed, Mr. Draper having retired from the leadership in favor of Mr. Henry Sherwood, and amongst other new members was Mr. John A. Macdonald, who had accepted the post of Receiver-General. At the close of this session Mr. Draper was honored with a judgeship, and rising from one judicial dignity to another, he at length achieved the highest place on the Canadian Bench—the Presidency of the Court of Error and Appeal. He died in 1877. The Sherwood-Daly Government was overwhelmingly defeated at the general election held early in 1848, and the Baldwin-Lafontaine Ministry returned to power. Amongst the members of the new House were William Hume Blake (father of Hon. Edward Blake) and Louis Joseph Papineau, who, from 1809 until his banishment for complicity in the rebellion of 1838, had been an influential leader of the Lower Canadians. He had been permitted to return to Canada in 1843, but his distrust of British rule and his wild project of a Canadian Republic were in no respect abated. In the House of Assembly he soon arrayed himself in deadly opposition to the Cabinet, denouncing "Responsible Government" in unmeasured terms. The adoption of the Free Trade policy in England at this time had a depressing effect upon Canadian commerce, as Canada ceased to be as heretofore the highway of American exports to the English markets. The result of this was the growth of a sentiment in favor of annexation. Parliament next met on the 18th of January, 1849, when Mr. George Etienne Cartier and Alexander Galt made their first appearance as members. Early in the session an Amnesty Bill in favor of those expelled from the country through the rebellion of '37-8 was passed. Under this measure Mr. Wm. Lyon Mackenzie returned to Canada from his exile in the United States. Besides this Bill, some two hundred more or less important measures were passed, amongst them being the Act reorganizing the Court of Chancery. While this Bill was regarded as an inestimable boon by all concerned, it was the means of closing the promising political career of Mr. Hume Blake, who, in deference to the wishes of his colleagues and of the legal profession of the Province, accepted the Chancellorship. The great measure of the session, from the historical point of view, was the Rebellion

Losses Bill. This measure was intended to supplement the compensation already granted by the Provincial Assemblies of Upper and Lower Canada to loyal citizens who had suffered loss by the rebellion of 1837-8. The legislation referred to had not recognized the cases of many whose property had been destroyed or damaged, not by rebels, but by those acting ostensibly in support of the authorities. This further relief was granted by an Act passed in the first session of the Union Parliament, but was restricted to Upper Canada. The Bill now passed extended the provisions for compensation to Lower Canada as well. Commissioners had been appointed by the Draper Government in 1845 to investigate and report upon the amount of money which would be required to settle the claims indicated, but great difficulty had been encountered in distinguishing between claimants who were entitled to relief and those who had been implicated more or less seriously in the rebellion. The report of the Commissioners was therefore not such as to afford a safe basis for legislation, and the Government, owing nothing to the Lower Canadians on the score of political support, had taken no further action. The Lafontaine-Baldwin Government felt that they were in duty bound to carry out the measure of justice which the former Government had initiated, and the French influence had now become strong enough to compel this even if the Government had felt otherwise. The Bill as passed expressly excluded from participation in the indemnity all rebels under the description of those "who had been convicted of treason or had been transported to Bermuda." It was reasonably believed that after the lapse of so many years, it would be impracticable to make any distinctions between "loyal citizens" and "rebels" apart from the record of the courts of law. The Opposition insisted, however, that such distinction *must* be made: and that no person who had taken part in the rebellion, whether convicted or not, should on any account be paid for his losses. The whole Conservative party took this "high loyal" ground, and the Bill at once evoked the most furious enmity in that quarter. The measure was debated in the House with unexampled passion—its chief opponents there being Mr. Sherwood, Col. Gugy, Sir Allan MacNab and Col. Prince; and its ablest defender Mr. Wm. Hume Blake, whose speech is justly regarded as the greatest effort of his life and the most powerful address ever delivered in the Canadian Parliament. The Bill was finally carried on March 9th by a majority of forty-seven to eighteen. Meantime the Tory party throughout the Province had poured in petitions to the Governor-General, demanding the reservation of the Bill or a dissolution of the House. After careful consideration, Lord Elgin could not see that his duty lay in either of these directions, and he accordingly assented to the measure amongst others on Wednesday, April 25th. As he retired from the Council Chamber after this ceremony, he was greeted with groans and hisses by a mob assembled in front of the building, and as his carriage rolled away it was pelted with rotten eggs. This incident is referred to in the first cartoon from *Punch in Canada* imbedded in our letter-press. In the evening of the same day a crowd assembled on the Champ-de-Mars, where "loyal speeches," openly advocating violence, were made. The mob was in a fitting frame of mind, and was swift to act upon the ill-advice. Amidst shouts and curses, an advance was made upon the Houses of Parliament. The legislators, engaged in discussing an important measure at the moment, were startled by the crashing in of the windows, and soon the rioters entered the chamber where, with maniacal fury, they demolished everything that was breakable, and wound up the peculiar display of "fealty to the Crown" by setting fire to the buildings. The Assembly House was totally consumed, involving a direct money loss far exceeding the amount appropriated by the Bill which had afforded the pretext for the outrage. Parliament assembled the next day in a chamber improvised in the Bonsecours market building. Sir Allan MacNab and a few of his political colleagues spoke in justification of the riot, and declared that the blame rested more with the Government than with the mob (see Cartoon 1). The members of the Ministry and many of their leading supporters were for several days maltreated on the streets, and the residences of Mr. Lafontaine and others in Montreal were wrecked by the mob. The carnival of "Loyalty" was kept up until the 30th when it culminated in a second and still more disgraceful attack upon Lord Elgin, on the occasion of an official visit to the Government House on Notre Dame street. After this outrage Lord Elgin remained in seclusion at Monklands for many months, earning thereby the sobriquet of the Hermit (see Cartoon 4). Parliament was prorogued on May 30th, Major General Rowan, Commander of the Forces, being commissioned to act for the Governor-General, who thought it best to avoid another demonstration of the "loyalists." The Government re-appointed the Draper Commissioners to carry out the provisions of the Rebellion Losses Bill in the adjudication of claims, and instructions were given them to use all possible care to distinguish between "rebels" and "loyalists" amongst the claimants, but this conciliatory action passed for little with the Tory press.

COLONEL GUGY'S POLITICAL TOY.

(*From Punch in Canada.*)

During the vacation, Sir Allan MacNab and Hon. Wm. Cayley proceeded to England to place the Tory view of the Rebellion Losses Bill before the public there; and about the same time Mr. Francis Hincks crossed the ocean on a similar errand for the Liberal party. Lord Elgin's course in the matter was ultimately sustained in both Houses of the Imperial Parliament when the subject came up for consideration. Subsequent riotous demonstrations in Montreal decided the question of the removal of the seat of Government from that city. The remaining two sessions were accordingly held in Toronto, and thereafter it was arranged to transfer the honor alternately to Quebec and Toronto every four years. The removal to Toronto took place in November, 1849, and the official residence was fixed at Elmsley Villa, on the site of the present Central Presbyterian Church.

As an outcome of the prevailing commercial depression of the time the project of annexation to the United States had come prominently forward for discussion, and in October a manifesto in favor of a peaceful separation from the Mother Country and a union with the Republic was published at Montreal. Amongst the signers of this celebrated document were many prominent persons connected with both political parties, amongst the number being Mr. Benjamin Holmes, to whom reference is made in this connection in the *Punch in Canada* cartoons. Mr. Papineau earnestly advocated the scheme, in consistence with his long cherished republican opinions, and many other public men—amongst them Col. Gugy—were suspected of sympathy with the movement. The only practical result of the agitation was to deprive some of those implicated in it of offices which they held at the pleasure of the Crown.

COLONEL GUGY'S NEW POSITION.

(*From Punch in Canada.*)

The next great questions to press for settlement were those relating to the Secularization of the Clergy Reserves and the abolition of Seigniorial Tenure—questions which concerned the Upper and Lower Provinces respectively. The first of these had its rise in the blunder originally made by the Imperial authorities in setting apart a large portion of the public domain for the maintenance of "a Protestant clergy." As population increased and settlement spread, the lands thus apportioned in various parts of the country—particularly those in Upper Canada—became valuable, and a hot dispute as to their ownership naturally arose. The Church of England laid exclusive claim to the term "Protestant Clergy," and, as a consequence, to the Reserves. The other denominations opposed these pretensions. At length, in 1840, an Imperial Act, intended to settle the question finally, decreed that the proceeds of all sales of reserved lands to date should be divided between the churches of England and Scotland,—the former body to receive two-thirds and the latter one-third; and that all future proceeds from such sales should be handed over, in the proportion of one-third and one-sixth, to the same churches; the residue to be devoted to the cause of public worship and religious instruction generally—in other words, to be divided, as might be, amongst such of the other Protestant denominations as cared to apply for it. This Act quite failed to allay the sense of injustice in regard to the Reserves, and the matter continued in agitation. In 1844 many supporters of the Reform party insisted on the question being made a political issue, and called upon the Government to petition the Home authorities for the repeal of the Act of 1840 as a preliminary to a radical settlement of the difficulty by the complete secularization of the Reserves. The Government failed to respond to this suggestion, and in 1849 a number of influential Reformers protested against the delay by stepping out of the Government ranks and forming a new organization, which became known by the *sobriquet* of the "Clear Grit" party. About the same time a somewhat similar departure was made by a number of French Liberals, who formed *Le Parti Rouge* under the leadership of Mr. Papineau. These new organizations joined in the advocacy of several advanced measures of reform, though the *Rouges* were on many points far more radical than the "Grits." When the session of 1850 opened, the Government found themselves confronted by an opposition not to be despised either in numbers or influence, aside from Conservatives, led by Sir Allan MacNab, John A. Macdonald, Wm. Cayley and Henry Sherwood. An incident of the session (to which reference is made in the caricature from *Punch in Canada* annexed) was the defection from the Conservative ranks of Col. Gugy, who had long been known as an ultra Tory. The reason assigned for this step by the hon. gentleman was his disapproval of the extreme rancor displayed during the opening debate by Sir Allan MacNab towards his political opponents, on issues which were practically dead, and to aspersions cast by that gentleman upon the Governor-General in connection with the events of 1837-8. The Clear Grits vigorously attacked the Government for their procrastination in the matter of the Clergy Reserves, and advocated the immediate passage of a Bill, without waiting for the formality of the repeal of the Imperial Act. It was evident that the Cabinet were by no means of one mind on this important question, and these passionate appeals were unheeded. The pressure was great enough, however, to ensure the passage of a resolution in favor of the repeal of the Act, and in due course an Address in accordance therewith was forwarded to the Imperial authorities. The attitude of the Ministry, however, was not definite enough to meet the views of the Reform Party at large, and the consequence was many defections from the ranks. Amongst warm friends who had been transformed to lukewarmness, was Mr. George Brown. The *Globe*, which had ridiculed the "Clear Grit" movement from its inception, was now preparing to cast in its fortunes with that faction. The next year was notable for the re-entry into Parliament of William Lyon Mackenzie, the hero of the Rebellion of '38. He was elected as member for Haldimand, having defeated Mr. Brown, who as yet professed a certain amount of friendship for the

Government. Mackenzie, of course, entered the House as their pronounced opponent, and soon became the clearest of Clear Grits. During the session of this year (1851) an Act was introduced by Hon. Mr. Hincks to make provision for the construction of a trunk line of railway from Quebec to the west. A guaranteed loan from the Home Government—such as had already been promised to Nova Scotia in promotion of a line from Halifax to Quebec, was anticipated. The outcome of this Act, some years later, was the Grand Trunk railway. Before the close of the session the *Globe* had reached the point of open hostility to the Government, and clamored for immediate action on the Clergy Reserves question. As yet, however, Mr. Brown was not in actual alliance with the Clear Grits. One of the planks in the platform of that party was the abolition of the Court of Chancery, which, as has been mentioned, was re-organized and established under Mr. Baldwin's auspices in 1849. Toward the end of the session, Mr. Lyon Mackenzie introduced a resolution looking to the abolition of this Court, and although defeated on a division, the fact that a majority of the Upper Canada members had voted in favor of the motion affected Mr. Baldwin so keenly that he resigned his office and retired from the Cabinet. Before the end of the same year Mr. Lafontaine also resigned, in pursuance of his expressed intention of retiring from public life. This act was immediately followed by the resignation of the remaining ministers, and the Lafontaine-Baldwin Cabinet thus passed calmly out of existence. Mr. Lafontaine was raised to the Bench as Chief Justice of Quebec in 1853, and the next year was created a Baronet. He died at Montreal, Feb. 26, 1864. Mr. Baldwin was defeated in North York at the ensuing general election by Mr. Joseph Hartman, a Clear Grit candidate, and this respected leader then permanently retired from public life. In 1854 he was made a C. B. The late Ministry having practically fallen before the Reform spirit of the day, the demand was for a Cabinet still less conservative. The formation of such a Cabinet was entrusted to Mr. (now Sir Francis) Hincks, who had been a prominent member of the late Administration, and was regarded as one of the most capable public men of the time. In a few months Mr. Hincks had completed the task committed to him by making judicious concessions to the Clear Grit sentiment and to all other forces which were capable of retarding the course of legislation. Mr. Morin, being the acknowledged leader of the French Liberals since the retirement of Mr. Lafontaine, headed the Lower Canada branch of the Government, which is known in our history as the Hincks-Morin Administration. The *Globe* came out strongly against the new Premier, expressing a total want of confidence in the sincerity of his Reform professions, and charging him with surrendering to French Canadian influence. The cause of the Government was on the other hand ably advocated by the Toronto *North American* (edited by Mr. Wm. Macdougall) and the Montreal *Pilot*, a journal established some years previously by Mr. Hincks himself. During the general election (1851) Mr. Brown was returned as member for Kent, and at once became a conspicuous figure in the House at Quebec—whither, in accordance with the alternating system, the seat of Government had been removed. Early in the new year Mr. Hincks proceeded to England, in company with Mr. E. B. Chandler of New Brunswick, to arrange for the Imperial guarantee to the construction of the Intercolonial railway, which, it had been agreed, should be built by the three Provinces of Quebec, New Brunswick and Nova Scotia, to connect Halifax and Quebec by way of the St. John Valley. The Home authorities expressed a preference for a military route around the shore, and declined the guarantee on any other condition. Though unsuccessful in this matter, Mr. Hincks succeeded, during his stay in England, in arranging for the formation of what is now known as the Grand Trunk railway company, to secure the early construction of the line westward from Montreal. On the Premier's return to Canada in 1852, the session opened, and Mr. Brown took the earliest opportunity of expressing his opinion that the Government was Reform in name only. Mr. John A. Macdonald also attacked them sharply, alleging that there was no principle in common among members of the Administration except the desire to hold office. During the session Mr. Hincks introduced a series of resolutions strongly urging the repeal of the Clergy Reserves Act of 1840, and an Address founded upon them was forwarded to the Queen. In October of this year Mr. Narcisse Fortunat Belleau (the subject of one of our cartoons) received a seat in the Legislative Council. Parliament adjourned on account of the presence of cholera at Quebec, between Nov. 10, 1852, and Feb. 14th, 1853. During this recess a despatch from the Home Secretary announced the intention of the Imperial Government to repeal the Act of 1840, and to pass an Act authorizing the Canadian Parliament to deal with the Clergy Reserves question. On the re-assembling of the House a Representation Act was passed, increasing the membership from 84 to 130— 65 for each section of the Province. About the same time it became known in Canada that the promised legislation in the matter of the Clergy Reserves had been passed in England, and the ardent advocates of secularization renewed their agitation for immediate action by the Provincial Government. The session was allowed to end, however, without any intimation of the Government's intentions, and this apparent want of good faith, in connection with various charges of extravagance in connection with railway contracts, and other shortcomings, furnished an abundance of ammunition for the Opposition in the interim. The Ministry decided to take no action on the Clergy Reserves question, the reason assigned being that it would be better to leave such important legislation to the next Parliament, in which there would be a larger representation of the people. This resolve, when announced in Parliament, raised a furious storm amongst the extreme members of the Opposition. No fewer than four amendments were moved to the Address in Reply, and the defeat of the Government was practically accomplished on a vote regretting that a measure for the settlement of the Seigniorial Tenure and Reserves question was not to be submitted during the session. This motion was carried by forty-two against twenty-nine. Mr. Hincks asked for an adjournment for a day or two, which was granted. The Ministry decided to dissolve the House, and when the members reassembled, Black Rod forthwith knocked at the door. The general election came off in the following July and August. Amongst the members of the new House subsequently noticed in our cartoons were Messrs. Luther Hamilton Holton and A. A. Dorion. The Assembly was now divided into three distinct parties: Ministerialists; Conservatives, led nominally by Sir A. MacNab,— really by Mr. John A. Macdonald; and Advanced Reformers, including Clear Grits and *Rouges*. Mr. Brown was now, to all intents and purposes, not only an ally but a leader of the last named party, with Mr. Dorion for his Lower Canada colleague. The Ministry managed to weather the storm for but a few days after the opening of the session; they were then defeated by a vote on a question of privilege raised by the Opposition, and handed in their resignations. This was on Sept. 8th, 1854. Sir Allan MacNab was called upon to form an Administration, a task which was only possible of accomplishment by the sacrifice on his part of cherished convictions at the bidding of expediency. The Government to be formed had before it the work of secularizing the Reserves, and to this Sir Allan, in common with the old Conservatives whom he represented, was opposed. Rather, however, than yield the leadership to the hands of his rising colleague, Macdonald, Sir Allan accepted the responsibility, and in due time completed the formation of a Government by an alliance of Conservatives and moderate French Liberals, with two representatives of the ministerial party nominated by Mr. Hincks. This Government, taking the names of the leaders of the two sections as was customary, is known as the MacNab-Morin Administration. The immediate secularization of the Reserves was an essential condition of the coalition, and the passage of a Bill abolishing the Seigniorial Tenure had also been stipulated for. With the advent of the new Cabinet, the old Tory Party may be said to have become extinct, as the leading colleagues of the new Premier were imbued with the prevailing spirit of progress to an extent which would almost entitle them to the name of Liberals. That title was, indeed, adopted, and the party in question has ever since been known as Liberal-Conservative. The old time Reform Party became similarly modified, by the absorption of its more conservative element into the ranks of Government supporters and of its radical members into the Clear Grit or *Rouge* party. The pledges of the Government as to the Reserves question were duly fulfilled by the introduction of the Secularization Act by Mr. John A. Macdonald in 1854. During the same session, the Seignioral Tenure system, a long-standing grievance of Lower Canada—a remnant of mediævalism, under which the tillers of the soil were practically the vassals of feudal lords—was also abolished. Upon the prorogation of Parliament Lord Elgin retired from the Governor-Generalship, and was succeeded by Sir Edmund Head. By a reconstruction of the Lower Canada section of the Cabinet during the recess, Mr. Geo. E. Cartier became Provincial Secretary. This is noteworthy, as marking the commencement of the long-continued comradeship in office of that gentleman with Mr. J. A. Macdonald. After another brief session at Quebec, the seat of Government was removed to Toronto. Meantime (in 1855) Mr. Hincks, while absent in England, received the appointment of Governor of Barbadoes and the Windward Islands and his connection with Canadian affairs thus ended for the time being. The questions of Separate Schools for Roman Catholics, and Representation by Population, were the important topics of political discussion next to be brought forward, but before they had become ripe for legislative action, an important change had taken place in the Ministry. The colleagues and supporters of the Government had become impatient of the nerveless leadership of Sir Allan MacNab, and anxious to replace him by an abler man, who stood ready for the position in the person of Mr. John A. Macdonald. Sir Allan MacNab, however, would not voluntarily resign, and the affairs of the Government were thus kept in a awkward state of suspense for a considerable time. The "conspirators" in the Cabinet at last succeeded in carrying their point. A resolution of confidence having been moved on the question of making Quebec the permanent seat of Government, the vote was taken, and it was found that although duly carried, a majority of the Upper Canada members had voted against it. This was seized upon as a pretext and, on a profession of adherence to the principle of a "double majority" (a principle which had never been adopted by either party), the Ministers handed in their resignations. This left Sir Allan alone in his glory, and he being unable to fill the vacant places. Col. Taché, as the senior Executive Councillor, was entrusted with the task of forming a ministry, which he speedily accomplished by replacing the members of the late Cabinet. Mr. Macdonald was made Attorney-General West, and was the actual leader (May, 1856). On a motion of no confidence moved by Mr. Dorion, the reconstructed ministry found the adverse Upper Canada majority increased, but having got rid of old Sir Allan they were not now so particular about the double majority "principle" and entertained no thought of resigning. For some time prior to 1856 Mr. Wm. Macdougall, as editor of the *North American*, had been agitating the question of the Hudson's Bay Company's possessions in the North-West. The project of obtaining control of that valuable domain for Canada now began to take shape, and was warmly advocated by many of the leading public men. Communications on the subject were opened with the Company, and early in 1857, Chief Justice Draper was sent over to England to represent the Province in the negotiations. During the Parliamentary session of the same year Mr. George Brown introduced a resolution in favor of the principle of

Representation by Population, which, although defeated, received strong support in the House and throughout the country. The vexed question of the permanent seat of Government was avoided by the submission of the matter to Her Majesty, who, in due course, named Ottawa, as a compromise between the conflicting claims of Toronto and Quebec. By the retirement of Col. Taché, which took place this year, Mr. Macdonald became Premier, and Mr. Cartier was formally appointed leader of the Lower Canada section of the Government. Parliament was dissolved in November and the general election came off in December and January. It was during this campaign that Mr. George Brown contested Toronto against Mr. John Beverley Robinson and others—reference to which is made in cartoons 17 to 24. Amongst the new members elected were Messrs. T. D'Arcy McGee, Hector L. Langevin, Christopher Duncan, Oliver Mowat, Wm. P. Howland, and John Carling. The main questions upon which the elections turned were Separate Schools and Representation by Population, and the general result was a weakening of the Upper Canada support of the Government and a more than proportionate addition to their Lower Canada following. When the House met in 1858, the "double majority" doctrine was promptly cast overboard, as it was clear the Ministry had to rely wholly on a Lower Canada majority. A motion expressing dissatisfaction with the selection of Ottawa as seat of Government, which appealed alike to the French and English members of the House, was carried by sixty-four to fifty. Thereupon the Government resigned, and Mr. George Brown was called upon, as leader of the Opposition, to form an Administration. This he succeeded in doing. He asked, however, for a dissolution of the House and an appeal to the country, on the ground that the present Assembly did not fairly represent public opinion. The Governor-General, upon consideration, declined to accede to this, and a vote of no confidence having been carried in the House, Mr. Brown and his colleagues handed in their resignations. The lately deposed ministers were recalled, and, taking advantage of the letter of the law which permitted of an interchange of portfolios without an appeal to the country, Mr. Macdonald and his colleagues performed what is notorious in our annals as the "Double Shuffle." The members of the Government resumed the treasury benches upon making a mere re-distribution of the offices. Having been duly sworn in, they then made another re-distribution which left them in the positions which they originally occupied.

The rejection of the double majority principle, and the popular demand for representation by population had given rise to the idea of a Federal Union of the Provinces of British North America, and the "new" Government announced that the feasibility of this scheme would receive the most serious consideration. Mr. A. T. Galt, who was now Inspector-General, was known as a strong advocate of Confederation, and on entering the Ministry he had insisted on it being made a Cabinet question. In the next session Ottawa was formally accepted as the seat of Government by a motion in the House, which was carried by a majority of five. A new Tariff Act, raising the general duties to fifteen per cent., was amongst the measures of the session, and marks the commencement of Protection in Canada.

At the close of the session the departments were once more established at Quebec, whence in 1866 they were removed to Ottawa and permanently settled in the new Parliament buildings. The Government was now sustained entirely by Lower Canada votes, and the cry of French domination was being vociferously raised in the Upper Province. As the outcome of a Liberal convention an address to the people made its appearance in 1860. This document, which forcibly exposed the unsatisfactory state into which public affairs had been brought by the existing system, was widely distributed, and is regarded as having done much to pave the way for the Confederation scheme subsequently matured. The Liberal leaders of Lower Canada were disposed to admit the justice of the complaints thus formulated, but no great expression of sympathy could be expected in that quarter for a cause with which the name of George Brown was intimately associated. In the meantime, the divisions in the ranks of the Opposition aided the Government. In the following session (1860) Mr. Brown introduced two motions embodying the reforms discussed at the convention, and suggesting, as a remedy for the evils complained of, the formation of local governments for the management of Provincial affairs, with some central authority to take cognizance of affairs common to all sections. These resolutions were defeated by overwhelming majorities. In connection with changes in the *personnel* of the Parliamentary forces during 1860, it may be noted that Sir Allan MacNab was elected to a seat in the Legislative Council, and Mr. Chas. J. Rykert succeeded Mr. Merritt as member for Lincoln in the Assembly. The agitation for "Rep. by Pop." and its proposed accompanying reforms was not allowed to die out. Mr. D'Arcy McGee continued to eloquently advocate the Federal Union plan, and the *Globe* kept steadily educating public opinion upon the subject. In the next session resolutions in favor of the "double majority" principle, moved respectively by Mr. J. Sandfield Macdonald and Mr. A. A. Dorion, obtained a fair measure of support in the House, being defeated by majorities of only thirteen and nineteen. Amongst the supporters of these motions were several prominent French Canadians who had hitherto acted with the Government, and ere long an alliance between these gentlemen and the Upper Canada followers of Mr. J. S. Macdonald was brought about, much to the embarrassment of the Ministry. The publication of the returns of the census, which had just been completed, gave new life to the agitation for Rep. by Pop. as they showed that the population of the Upper Province was 300,000 in excess of that of Lower Canada. A measure embodying to some extent the principles contended for was, however, defeated by a vote of sixty-seven to forty-nine. On the 10th of June

Parliament was dissolved, and at the ensuing general election the Government was sustained, notwithstanding the herculean efforts of the Opposition. Mr. Brown himself was defeated in East Toronto, and Mr. Dorion failed in Lower Canada. Mr. Brown remained out of Parliament until 1863; Mr. Dorion was returned for Hochelaga in the year following his defeat. Amongst the new members (subsequently noticed in our cartoons) were Alexander Mackenzie and H. G. Joly. Mr. Mackenzie was elected for Lambton, and has remained in Parliament to the present time. M. Joly sat as member for Lotbinière. Mr. Wm. Lyon Mackenzie, who had resigned his seat for Haldimand in 1858, died during the summer of this year.

Sir Edmund Head's term having expired, he was succeeded in the Governorship by Viscount Monck. In 1862 Mr. John Beverley Robinson and Mr. John Carling became members of the Cabinet, the former as President of the Council, and the latter as Receiver-General. Both of these gentlemen (who figure in several of our cartoons) were favorable to Rep. by Pop., and that question was henceforth to be regarded as "open" in the Cabinet. The Ministerial span of life was, however, now at an end. Before the session closed the Government sustained a decisive defeat on a militia bill introduced by Attorney-General Macdonald, and resigned on the following day. The Macdonald-Sicotte Administration succeeded to the vacant benches, the Premier being Mr. John Sandfield Macdonald, and his Lower Canadian colleague, Mr. L. V. Sicotte, a former follower of Mr. Cartier. The new Ministry, in announcing their programme, practically ignored the question of Rep. by Pop., and adopted the principle of Separate Schools. In the following session Mr. George Brown (who had meantime been elected for South Oxford) found himself at the head of a strong party in opposition to the Government on the issues named, and although the "double majority" principle was supposed to have been adopted by the Ministry, they resisted defeat on many divisions by a solid Lower Canada vote. Indeed, in this respect they were in precisely the same position as the Government they had replaced. This disingenuous conduct brought swift punishment. The Government was in May defeated on a direct vote of want of confidence, and a dissolution was decided upon. The general election was fixed for June, and resulted in the Government being sustained. The *personnel* of the Cabinet had undergone some changes in the meantime. Mr. Oliver Mowat being taken in as Postmaster-General, and the Lower Canada section being as follows: A. A. Dorion, L. H. Holton, Isidore Thibaudeau, L. Letellier de St. Just, L. S. Huntington and Maurice Laframboise. Mr. Huntington was comparatively new to Parliament, and represented Shefford. In the second session after its formation this Government voluntarily resigned office, being unable to command a working majority, and in the meantime little if any progress had been made toward the settlement of the great question of the day. After some difficulty a new Government was formed under the joint leadership of Sir E. P. Taché and Hon. John A. Macdonald. In this Cabinet Mr. Hector L. Langevin first sat as a Minister; the new names in the Upper Canada section were those of Messrs. John Simpson and James Cockburn. It was found, on the reassembly of Parliament, that this Government, like its predecessor, could not command a working majority, and it was evident that no Ministry it would be possible to form from the material available would be in any better position. It had been decided to dissolve the House and appeal to the country, when, at the critical moment, Mr. George Brown suggested that the crisis might be utilized to settle the constitutional difficulties between Upper and Lower Canada on the line of the recommendations just laid before the House by a committee entrusted with the consideration of that subject, viz.: a Confederation of the Provinces.

PROPOSED WINDOW FOR THE PARLIAMENT BUILDING.

(*From Diogenes.*)

As the result of conferences then initiated a Federal Union of the Provinces was decided upon, and three Reformers, Messrs. Brown, Mowat and Macdougall entered the Government to assist in carrying the plan into effect.

In due course the Imperial authorities passed the necessary legislation, under the title of the British North America Act, and on the 1st of July, 1867, the plan was consummated, and the Dominion of Canada came into existence. For distinguished services in connection with this great measure, Mr. Macdonald was honored with knighthood, and in the following year Mr. Cartier accepted a baronetcy. Other distinguished Confederationists received minor honors. In the ensuing general election, Mr. Brown was defeated in South Ontario, and never thereafter sat in Parliament. In 1873 he accepted a seat in the Senate at the hands of the Reform Government of Mr. Mackenzie, and in that quiet retreat ended his eventful political career. The formation of Provincial Ministries had meantime been arranged for. In Ontario, the first Cabinet—a coalition—was under the leadership of Mr. John Sandfield Macdonald, and remained in office for the ensuing four years. Amongst the new Members of the first Dominion Parliament were Joseph Howe of Nova Scotia and Edward Blake of Ontario, the latter gentleman being at the same election (1867) returned as a member of the Ontario Assembly, where he soon assumed the leadership of the Opposition. Mr. Howe continued his active efforts against Confederation both in and out of the House. In 1868 he was the leading member of a delegation to England to present an address in favor of the repeal of the Union on behalf of Nova Scotia. This petition was rejected, and early in 1869 Mr. Howe was induced to enter the Cabinet, certain modifications of the terms of Union being promised. In 1868, Lord Monck was succeeded in the Governorship by Sir John Young (afterward Lord Lisgar). In the ensuing session, the North-West Territories, which had been acquired by the extinction of the Hudson's Bay Company's claim, were formally added to the Dominion, and an Act was passed to provide for the appointment of a Lieutenant-Governor and Council to administer their affairs. The closing negotiations in England had been conducted by Sir Geo. Cartier (Cartoon 32) and Hon. Wm. Macdougall, and in recognition of his services the latter gentleman was appointed Lieutenant-Governor of the new Territory. The Metis settlers, however, felt aggrieved that the transfer had been effected without their consent, and entertained a want of confidence in the good-will of the new owners of the country. The result was that when Lieutenant-Governor Macdougall undertook to assume the direction of affairs he was met by armed resistance, and found that the half-breeds about Fort Garry were in open rebellion under the leadership of one Louis Riel. Upon the peremptory order of the rebels Mr. Macdougall was forced to retreat from the frontier (Cartoon 49). Meanwhile the rebellion went on. Bishop Taché, a prelate of vast influence amongst the half-breeds, happened unfortunately to be absent in Rome. It being clear that peace could not be restored without his intervention, he was communicated with, and on his arrival at Ottawa he was empowered to offer the rebels an amnesty for all past offences and to assure them of the good-will of the Dominion. He at once departed on his mission, but before his arrival at the Red River, Riel had crowned his folly and wickedness by the cold-blooded murder of a loyalist named Thomas Scott, under form of a "court martial" execution. The Bishop, notwithstanding this, duly delivered his message. The rebels were ultimately overawed by the appearance of a military force under command of Colonel (afterwards Sir Garnet) Wolseley, and Riel took flight. He returned, however, after a time, and remained in Manitoba unmolested until the offer of a reward for his apprehension by the Ontario Government caused him to seek safety on the American side. To forestall further trouble the Dominion Government, at the suggestion of Bishop Taché, secretly provided him with some $1,500 on condition of his remaining out of the country for good. With this strangely acquired booty he took up his residence in the United States. He was subsequently twice elected to Parliament for the constituency of Provencher, Manitoba, but his banishment from the country for five years was decreed in connection with the general amnesty subsequently ratified by the Mackenzie Government.

In 1872 Sir John Macdonald was appointed one of the British Commissioners for the arrangement of a treaty involving the fishery interests of Canada, amongst other important matters, as between Great Britain and the United States. The result of the Commissioners' labors is known as the Washington Treaty, which was ratified in that year. By this document, *inter alia*, the right to take fish in Canadian waters was extended to the United States for the period of ten years in consideration of a money payment, the amount subsequently agreed upon by a joint Commission, which met at Halifax in 1877, being $5,500,000. This the Americans paid, but only after a protest on flimsy grounds by their representative, Mr. Kellogg, and much grumbling by Congress. In 1871, British Columbia was admitted to the Union. In the session of the following year a Bill was passed empowering the Government to contract with a chartered company for the construction of a railway to connect British Columbia with the Eastern Provinces. This year was also signalized by the advent of Lord Dufferin as the successor of Baron Lisgar in the vice-regal office, and by a general election, the term of the first Parliament of the Dominion having expired. The result of the election was favorable to the Government, though the Opposition was materially strengthened. In 1873 Confederation was rounded off by the admission of Prince Edward Island into the Union. The session of this year is memorable for the "Pacific Scandal." Mr. Huntington from his place in the House charged the Government with having corruptly sold the contract for the construction of the C. P. R., to Sir Hugh Allan, in consideration of a large contribution by that worthy knight to the Conservative election fund. This unparalleled indictment caused a great sensation, and eventually compelled the resignation of the Ministry. A Reform Government under Mr. Mackenzie succeeded to office, and continued down to 1878, when the prevailing depression of trade compassed its defeat, the Conservatives having declared for Protection to native industries as a "National Policy," a cry which caught the public fancy wonderfully. The leading political incidents of the term thus briefly indicated are commented upon in their order in the cartoons from GRIP presented in this volume. Early in 1880, Mr. Mackenzie was succeeded in the leadership by Mr. Blake, who still remains at the head of the Reform Party.

THE MAN WOT FIRED THE PARLIAMENT HOUSE.

As a climax to the excitement which attended the passage of the Rebellion Losses Bill, the House of Parliament at Montreal was destroyed by incendiarism. This outrage was well-known to have been the act of a Party, but the individual hand that wielded the torch, was not known. *Punch in Canada*, the comic paper of the day, and a strong opponent of the measure in question, took advantage of this fact to suggest humorously that "the man wot fired the Parliament House" was Lafontaine—the man who led the Government in the matter which had so excited the Conservative wrath, and so led to the catastrophe.

PUNCH IN CANADA, MAY 19th, 1849.

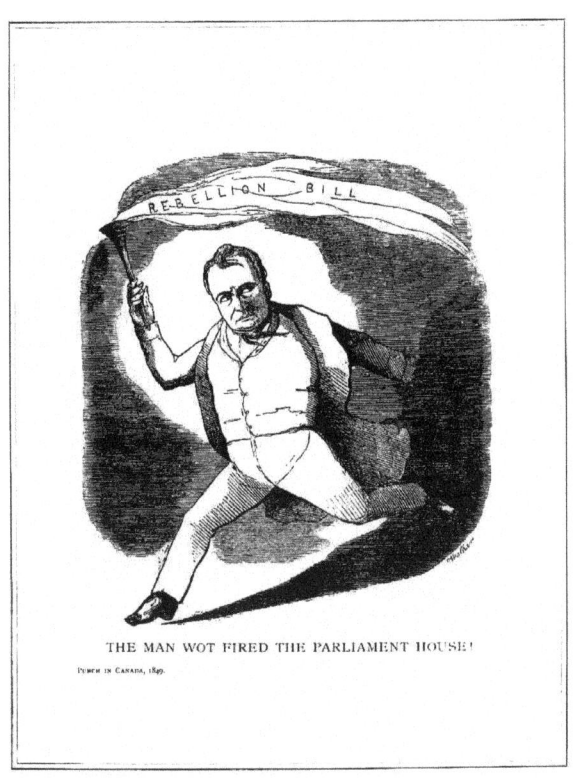

THE MAN WOT FIRED THE PARLIAMENT HOUSE!

PUNCH IN CANADA, 1849.

THE CLUB NATIONALE DEMOCRATIQUE PREPARING TO TRAMPLE ON THE BRITISH LION.

This was a satirical allusion to the "tall talk" indulged in by a coterie of French followers of Papineau, who favored a democratic form of Government for Canada as a cure for the prevailing discontent.

PUNCH IN CANADA, JULY 7th, 1849.

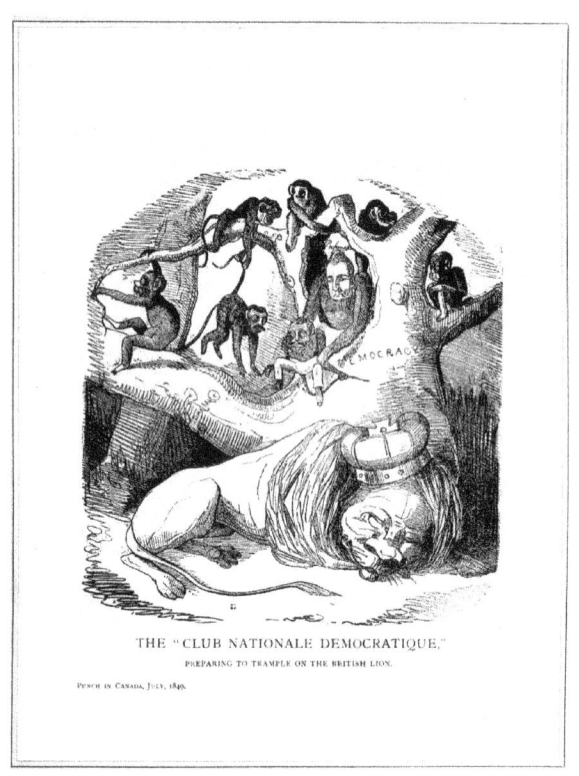

THE "CLUB NATIONALE DEMOCRATIQUE,"

PREPARING TO TRAMPLE ON THE BRITISH LION.

PUNCH IN CANADA, JULY, 1849.

SCENE AT BUCKINGHAM PALACE.

Sir Allan Macnab and Hon. Wm. Cayley visited England on behalf of the Conservative Party, to endeavor to influence public and Parliamentary opinion in connection with Canadian questions, which at the time were exciting unusual attention. Mr. Francis Hincks was sent over about the same time to represent the Reform view, and to counteract the influence of the gentlemen named.

PUNCH IN CANADA, JULY, 1849.

A SCENE AT BUCKINGHAM PALACE.

HER MOST GRACIOUS MAJESTY.—"Sir Allan Macnab and Mr. William Cayley,—I regret that it is out of our power to offer you any accommodations at present, our only spare room being just now occupied by Mr. Francis Hincks."

PUNCH IN CANADA, JULY 1849.

THE HERMIT.

Lord Elgin, the Governor-General, was criticised for secluding himself from society at the official residence, Monklands.

PUNCH IN CANADA, AUGUST, 1849.

THE HERMIT.

Lately discovered in the woods, near Monklands; and now about to be forwarded to England by the gentlemen of the British League, to whom this Portrait is respectfully dedicated.

PUNCH IN CANADA, AUGUST, 1849.

DROPPING A HINT.

Colonel Gugy, M.P., was a prominent member of the Opposition under the Baldwin-Lafontaine Ministry, but announced his withdrawal from that position during the heated scenes which followed the Rebellion Losses riots.

He is regarded as having been the progenitor of the Liberal-Conservative Party of the present time. The cartoon conveys the insinuation that Colonel Gugy sympathized with the Annexation movement, which was the sensation of the day.

PUNCH IN CANADA, MAY, 1849.

DROPPING A HINT.

BOY.—Hallo, Mister! ye've dropped yer hankercher.

LEAGUER.—Ha! my good boy, yes!—I mean no, my blessed little kid, no! not mine, my excellent little gentleman, not mine—Oh no, no, no, not mine!

BOY.—Well, some o' yis dropped it anyhow, and now none o' yiz 'll own to it.

PUNCH IN CANADA, MAY, 1849.

THE ANNEXATION ENGINE.

This was another attack upon the Annexation sentiment which prevailed in Lower Canada. Mr. Papineau is again the principal figure, and *Punch's* idea was that if Annexation were ever realized its first effect would be to rob the French-Canadians of the special privileges they enjoyed under British rule. The artist's conception of Brother Jonathan is somewhat unique.

PUNCH IN CANADA, 1849.

THE WAY BROTHER JONATHAN WILL ASTONISH THE NATIVES.
ANNEXATION COMES IN BY THE RAIL, WHILE LIBERTY FLIES OFF IN THE SMOKE.

PUNCH IN CANADA, 1849.

THE THIMBLERIG.

This cartoon appeared during the discussion of the removal of the Seat of Government from Montreal after the destruction of the old building at the hands of the mob. Hon. Robert Baldwin, who was Premier at the time, was supposed to favor his native place, Toronto, in the selection; Kingston and Montreal were the other competitors for the honor. Mr. *Punch* naturally gave Montreal the preference.

PUNCH IN CANADA, SEPTEMBER, 1849.

THE GOVERNMENT THIMBLERIG.

Here I am, Sporting Bob from York!—Rowl in here, gentlemen, and stake your money. Now, Mr. Sherwood! I see you looking at one of the thimbles;—

walk up, sir, like a man, and go your length upon it in gold or silver,—Debentures taken at a small discount. Here you are, Mr. What-d'ye-call him, the coroner from Kingston! Sport your jinglers here upon the lucky thimble;—a quick eye and a ready observation takes the tin. O, there's the French gentlemen from Montreal feeling for their purses!—step this way, gentlemen, and the day's your own. Rowl in.

(*Here Punch clandestinely tilts up a thimble, and discovers the pea.*)

PUNCH IN CANADA, SEPTEMBER, 1849.]

PAWNING THE FLAG.

Mr. Benjamin Holmes was one of the Members for Montreal in the first Parliament after the Union, and was amongst the most active public men of the time. In 1849 he was an advocate of Annexation, and subsequently voted for the reception of an address in favor of Canadian Independence. His Annexation proclivities are hit off in the cartoon, which represents him as pawning the British flag to Brother Jonathan.

PUNCH IN CANADA, OCTOBER 10th, 1849.

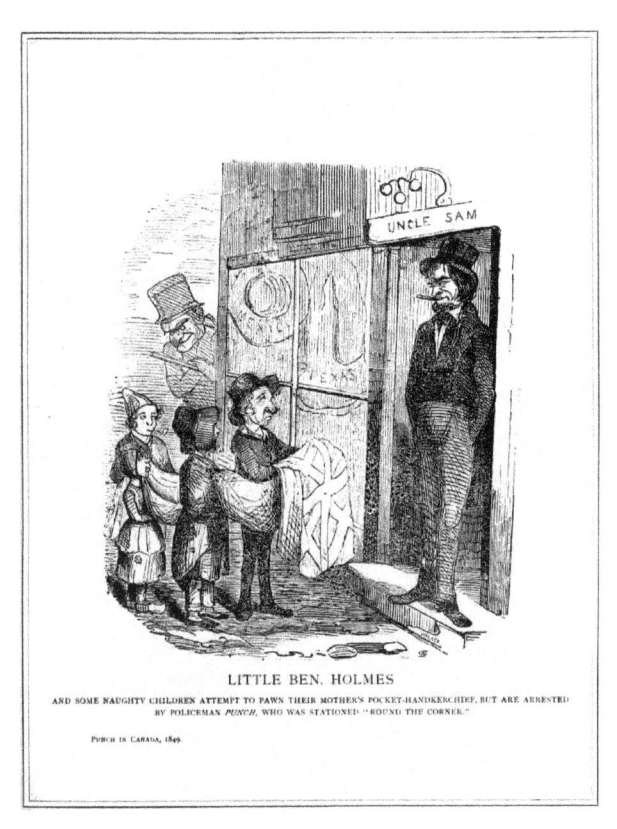

LITTLE BEN. HOLMES

AND SOME NAUGHTY CHILDREN ATTEMPT TO PAWN THEIR MOTHER'S POCKET-HANDKERCHIEF, BUT ARE ARRESTED BY POLICEMAN *PUNCH*, WHO WAS STATIONED "ROUND THE CORNER."

PUNCH IN CANADA, 1849.

THE EAGLE AND THE FAWN.

A piece of excusable self-glorification on the part of Mr. *Punch*, who was "truly loyal" from first to last. Here he dashes forth upon his charger to rescue the Canadian fawn from the talons of the designing American Eagle.

PUNCH IN CANADA, OCTOBER, 1849.

THE EAGLE AND THE FAWN.

Punch in Canada, October, 1849.

TWO YEARS AFTER ANNEXATION.

This satire is at the expense of Mr. Benjamin Holmes' infirmity in the matter of strong drink, while it also includes a hit at his Annexation record.

Punch in Canada, November, 1849.

TWO YEARS AFTER ANNEXATION.

UNCLE BEN.—BUY A BUST, SIR?—GENERAL WASHINGTON, SLIGHTLY DAMAGED, AND GOING VERY CHEAP.

PUNCH.—O, A "BUST," EH?—AH! YES, I THOUGHT IT WOULD COME TO A "BUST" WITH YOU BEFORE LONG.

PUNCH IN CANADA, NOVEMBER, 1849.

HERE WE ARE AND HERE WE GO.

The question of the removal of the Seat of Government having been decided in favor of Toronto, the cartoon affects to give a view of the removal itself under the similitude of a circus caravan. The figure upon the wagon in the foreground was no doubt intended to represent Lord Elgin, although no attempt was made to catch the likeness. The basket of eggs and the hen in close proximity are a sufficient hint as to the identity, Lord Elgin having been "rotten-egged" by a Montreal mob for signing the Rebellion Losses Bill.

PUNCH IN CANADA, NOVEMBER 29th, 1849.

CLOWN LOQUITER—HERE WE GO, AND HERE WE ARE.

PUNCH IN CANADA, NOVEMBER, 1849.

THE PUDDING AND THE WASP.

Mr. Henry John Boulton, M.P., for Niagara, was a somewhat prominent figure in the Canadian Parliament, in which he occupied an "independent" attitude. Toward the close of his Parliamentary career he was favorably

- 38 -

mentioned for appointment to the Judicial Bench, but the honor was withheld, chiefly through the opposition offered by the *Colonist*, an influential paper published at Toronto.

PUNCH IN CANADA, DECEMBER, 1849.

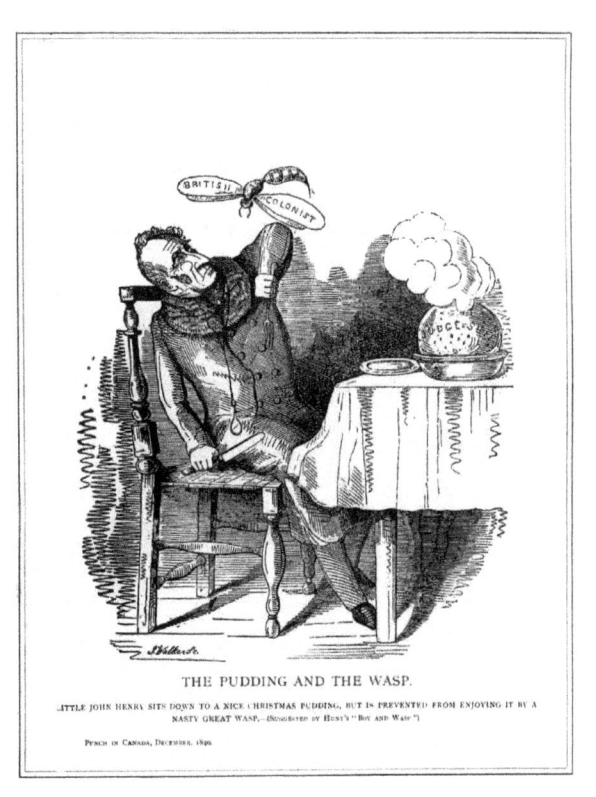

THE PUDDING AND THE WASP.

LITTLE JOHN HENRY SITS DOWN TO A NICE CHRISTMAS PUDDING, BUT IS PREVENTED FROM ENJOYING IT BY A NASTY GREAT WASP.—(SUGGESTED BY HUNT'S "BOY AND WASP")

PUNCH IN CANADA, DECEMBER, 1849.

THE TRAPPERS.

This cartoon signalizes the triumph of Toronto in being at last made the Seat of Government. Henry Sherwood and Robert Baldwin, the "trappers" of the picture, were prominent representatives of Toronto, though on opposite sides of politics, and both had urged the claims of their native city when the Government was first removed from Kingston. Elmsley Hut indicates the official residence, which was known as Elmsley House, on the site of the present Central Presbyterian Church. The "Beaver" in the case is, of course, Lord Elgin.

PUNCH IN CANADA, DECEMBER 28th, 1849.

THE TRAPPERS.

"I saw young Harry with his beaver," etc.—*Shakspeare.*

FIRST TRAPPER.—SAY, BOB, DARNED IF WE AIN'T KETCHED THE OLD HE BEAVER RIGHT INTO THE TRAP, AND THE OTHERS IS A-CROWDING ROUND LIKE ALL CREATION!

SECOND TRAPPER.—WELL, KEEP HIM THAR, BOY, KEEP HIM THAR: —I GUESS HE DON'T QUIT THIS CLEARIN JIST YIT. THIS IS SOME, THIS GAME IS:—DARNED IF IT DON'T BEAT HEUKER!

PUNCH IN CANADA, DECEMBER, 1849.]

TOWNSHIPS COLONIZATION—A SETTLER.

This was an allusion, from the English standpoint, to the unfitness of French emigrants as agricultural settlers. The contrast between the results of farming industry in Upper and Lower Canada seemed to justify this prejudice. The comparison of the newly-arrived Frenchman to the frogs is a time-honored joke, supposed to have arisen from the alleged French national taste for frogs'-legs as a table delicacy.

PUNCH IN CANADA, 1849.

TOWNSHIPS COLONIZATION—A SETTLER.

YOUNG LITERARY LEADER.—HERE IS ONE SETTLER, SARE, FOR YOUR TOWNSHIP, SARE, ON YOUR FARM, SARE.

TOWNSHIPPER.—OH, THAT'S YOUR SETTLER, EH? WHY THERE'S LOTS OF THEM CHAPS HERE ALREADY—IN THE MASHES!

PUNCH IN CANADA, 1849.

A WINTER'S TALE.

After the troubles of 1837, William Lyon Mackenzie became an exile from Canada. In the verses in the legend, he recounts his unhappy experiences in political life to Robert Baldwin, who is figuratively represented as bearing him company. The gallows on the mainland in the distance is a reminder that a price had been set upon Mackenzie's head.

PUNCH IN CANADA, 1849.

WINTER'S TALE.

AUTOLYCUS, — (*A Knavish Peddler*) — MR. W. L. MACKENZIE.

CLOWN, — — MR. BALDWIN.

AUTOLYCUS.—I see this is the time that the unjust man doth thrive. Sure the gods do this year connive at us, that we may do anything extempore. (*Sings.*)

1837.

The daisies were dead on Gallows Hill,—
With heigh! the skulkers behind the rail,—
O then I thought my pockets to fill!
For the red blood flowed and I robbed the mail.

1838.

The hemp-fields waving in the breeze—
With hey! the ravens. O how they croak!
And the birds that hung from the gallows-trees,
Might rede me then that it was no joke.

1849.

But now the lark tra lira sings!
A Navy-islander bold am I;
And sympathizers may plume their wings
All in the clover as they lie.

CLOWN.—He seems to be of great authority; close with him, give him gold.
PUNCH IN CANADA, 1849.

EFFECT OF TORONTO BEER AND BEEF, ETC.

It is not unlikely that there was some physical ground for this reference to Lafontaine, although the satirist's primary allusion is to the happy political effect of the calmer atmosphere in which the French leader was now living.
PUNCH IN CANADA, 1849.

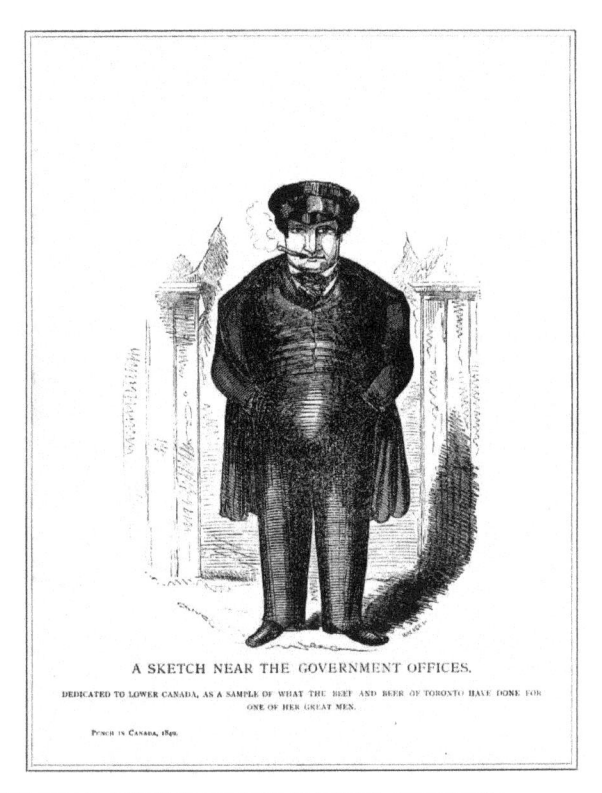

A SKETCH NEAR THE GOVERNMENT OFFICES.

DEDICATED TO LOWER CANADA, AS A SAMPLE OF WHAT THE BEEF AND BEER OF TORONTO HAVE DONE FOR ONE OF HER GREAT MEN.

Punch in Canada, 1849.

UP GOES THE DONKEY.

This was the first of a series of cartoons which appeared in Toronto, in 1858, in connection with the election contest between Mr. John Beverley Robinson and Mr. George Brown, for the representation of the city of Toronto in Parliament. Mr. Bowes was Mayor for several years. He was Mr. Robinson's "right hand man" in the campaign, though, with a not over-friendly hand the artist represents the candidate as occupying a secondary position throughout. This was the occasion of Mr. Robinson's first entry into parliamentary life.

This, and the five following cartoons are inserted as an illustration of the manner in which public questions were caricatured in those days.

FLY SHEET, 1858.

UP GOES THE DONKEY!

MR. BOWES TRIES A NEW DODGE.

BOWES BAGGING HIS GAME.

From what is known of the amenities of politics in those days, it is not unlikely that the charge of wholesale, open bribery, here made against the Conservative candidates, was well founded. The Conservatives were not so fortunate as to have a caricaturist on their side, or no doubt an equally faithful picture might have been levelled at Mr. Brown and his supporters.

FLYSHEET, 1857.

MR. BOWES BAGGING HIS GEESE (VOTES).

USED UP.

The despondency, here attributed to the Conservative candidate, is supposed, of course, to have resulted from the fact that Mr. Brown was on the popular side of the question then occupying public attention. He was also more than a match for his opponent on the platform by virtue of natural gifts.

FLYSHEET, 1857.

USED UP; OR, THE RETURN OF BOWES AND ROBINSON FROM THE NOMINATION.

BOWES AND HIS PETTICOATED FRIENDS.

Mr. Bowes appears to have enlisted the sympathies of the Roman Catholic hierarchy on the side of the Tory candidates by the usual means—glowing promises of special favors to that denomination.

FLYSHEET, 1857.

MR. BOWES AND HIS PETTICOATED FRIEND INTRODUCE THEIR CANDIDATE TO THE PEOPLE.

MR. BOWES AND HIS PETTICOATED FRIEND INTRODUCE THEIR CANDIDATE TO THE PEOPLE.

THE RAT TRAP.

This cartoon depicts the attempt to catch the Catholic votes by baiting the trap with the Tory candidate. Mr. George Brown was at this time exceedingly unpopular with the Roman Catholics, on account of his outspoken ultra-Protestantism in the *Globe*.

FLYSHEET, 1857.

THE RAT TRAP.

THE PETTICOATED GENTLEMAN FINDS THE ROBINSON BAIT DOES NOT TAKE.

THE SICK CANDIDATE.

As the campaign progressed this valiant artist-partizan of course descried signs of the complete collapse of Mr. Robinson.

FLYSHEET, 1857.

THE SICK CANDIDATE.

"BY THE HOLY ST. PATRICK, THE BARROW IS GIVING WAY, AND I SHALL HAVE TO LEAVE MY POOR ROBINSON IN THE MUD."

THE BROKEN PLANK.

The idea of the last cartoon is reiterated in another form. The discomfiture and defeat of the Conservative candidate is practically complete (in the artist's mind).

FLYSHEET, 1857.

THE BROKEN PLANK.

"THE GAME IS UP."

THE LAST KICK.

The cartoon, of course, appeared before the polling-day. The fact that Mr. Robinson was elected, as well as Mr. Brown, would seem to require a slight revision of the picture.

FLYSHEET, DECEMBER 22nd, 1857.

THE LAST KICK.

THE THREE MARTYRS.

Nine members of the Reform party, who were won over to the side of the Government of J. S. Macdonald (which was a coalition), were dubbed "the martyrs." This cartoon represents Mr. Macdonald in the act of compelling the ratification of the bargain with three of the number—Messrs. Lauder, Colcohoun, and Hamilton.

FLYSHEET, 1868.

THE AXE-GRINDER AND THE THREE TRAITORS.

THE AXE-GRINDER AND THE THREE TRAITORS.

THE NEEDY AXE-GRINDER.

Mr. John Sandfield Macdonald, who was at this time Premier of Ontario, earned the *sobriquet* of the Axe-Grinder by some self-descriptive expression he had made use of in a public speech. His political methods were largely based upon the *quid pro quo* principle.

FLYSHEET, 1868.

THE NEEDY AXE-GRINDER.

Needy Axe-Grinder, whither are you going?
Rough is the road, your wheel is out of order,
Bleak blows the blast, your hat has a hole in it,
So have your breeches.
Tell me, Axe-Grinder, how came you to grind axes?
Did some rich man tyrannically use you?
Was it John A.?

CROSS ROADS.

Dr. (now Sir) Chas. Tupper was a warm advocate of Confederation, and did more than any other public man to induce his native Province, Nova Scotia

(Acadia), to enter the Union in 1867. Hon. Joseph Howe, a much greater statesman than Tupper, and a man of vast influence, was amongst the opponents of the measure in question, and was suspected of a preference for annexation to the United States. In the cartoon the Province is represented as halting between the two opinions, and the loyal artist takes pains to point out that the advantages are all in the way that leads "to Ottawa."

DIOGENES, NOVEMBER 20th, 1868.

CROSS ROADS.

SHALL WE GO TO WASHINGTON FIRST, OR HOW(E)?

THE DOMINION COUNTING-HOUSE.

Referring to Hon. Joseph Howe's acceptance of a seat in the Dominion Government, as President of the Council, an action which was regarded by many of his Nova Scotia friends in the light of an apostacy. The other persons represented are Sir John Rose, Minister of Finance, and Sir John A. Macdonald.

DIOGENES, JANUARY 20th, 1869.

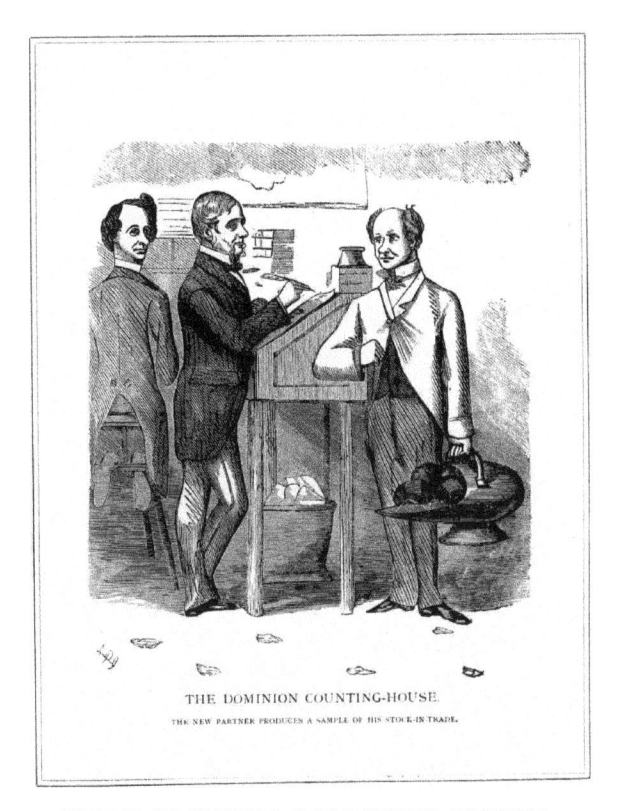

THE DOMINION COUNTING-HOUSE.

THE NEW PARTNER PRODUCES A SAMPLE OF HIS STOCK-IN-TRADE.

A SCENE IN THE QUEBEC CIRCLE.

This cartoon, which refers to matters of current interest in the Quebec Local House, was originally accompanied by the following rhyming comment:

Pity the sorrows of a little man[1]

Weighted with load beyond his puny power;

He does his best—the best a small man can—
But sinks, contorted, in the trying hour.

Chauveau would willingly bestow his aid,
But, all engrossed, stuffs Education "Bill;"
While Cauchon's grunt is heard from out the shade,
"Root, hog or die," he cries, "It is my will!"

> 1. Christopher Dunkin, whose name is associated with the well-known Dunkin Act of subsequent years.

DIOGENES, MARCH 19th, 1869.

A SCENE IN THE QUEBEC CIRCLE.

THE HAPPY PAIR.

Hon. Joseph Howe had relinquished his efforts in favor of the Repeal of Confederation after the rejection of the petition sent to England by the Nova Scotians, and had expressed a formal acceptance of the Union, prior to becoming a member of the Dominion Cabinet. This was exceedingly distasteful to his former Repeal allies in Nova Scotia, two of whom, Messrs. Wilkins and Annand, are represented in the cartoon. Mr. Howe's change of base was attributed to self interest in some quarters; the artist in turn assigns jealousy as the motive of his opponents.

DIOGENES, MARCH 26th, 1869.

THE HAPPY PAIR.

DIOGENES, (LOQ.)—"BLESS YOU, MY CHILDREN."

THE CANADIAN AUTOLYCUS.

A playful allusion to Sir George E. Cartier's well-known fondness for official life and its stately surroundings, in anticipation of the opening of the Session at Ottawa on April 15th.

DIOGENES, APRIL 2nd, 1869.

THE CANADIAN AUTOLYCUS.

Scene: OTTAWA. *Time:* A FORTNIGHT HENCE.

Autolycus—SIR G. E. C—T—R, Bart., (*loq.*)—"Whether it like me or no, I am a courtier. See'st thou not the air of the Court in these enfoldings? Hath not my gait in it the measure of the Court? Receives not thy nose Court odor from me? Reflect I not on thy baseness Court contempt. * * * I am courtier cap-a-pe; and one that will either push on or pluck back thy business there."—*The Winter Tale;—Act IV., Scene III.*

A DOMINION EASTER OFFERING.

Sir George E. Cartier had been a member of the Commission sent to England to negotiate for the transfer of the North-West Territory to the Dominion, and the surrender of the rights of the Hudson Bay Company. The successful result of the mission was now announced to Parliament. The conditions agreed upon involved a payment by the Dominion Government of £300,000.

DIOGENES, APRIL 16th, 1869.

A DOMINION EASTER OFFERING.

MISS CANADA.—"THANK YOU, SIR GEORGE! I'VE BEEN WAITING FOR HIM SUCH A LONG TIME! BUT DON'T YOU THINK, AFTER ALL, HE MAY PROVE RATHER TROUBLESOME?"

AXES TO GRIND.

To those who understand what is ordinarily expected of a man who controls patronage, by his political "friends," the meaning of this sketch will be sufficiently obvious. Sir George E. Cartier was not exempt from the penalties of such a position.

DIOGENES, APRIL 23rd, 1869.

"AXES TO GRIND."

SIR GEORGE, (LOQ.)—"TAKE YOUR TIME, GENTLEMEN, SOME OF YOUR METAL IS PRETTY HARD."

TOO OLD TO BE CAUGHT WITH CHAFF.

This was intended as a tribute to the unquestionable loyalty of Sir John Macdonald, as opposed to the alleged annexation proclivities of Mr. Lucius Seth Huntington (afterwards Postmaster-General in the Mackenzie Government), and other prominent men in the Eastern townships district.

DIOGENES, JUNE 4th, 1869.

"TOO OLD TO BE CAUGHT WITH CHAFF."

FARMER JOHN.—"IT'S NO USE YOU FELLOWS TRYING ON THAT GAME. IF YOU WANT HIM, YOU'LL HAVE TO PIT ANOTHER BIRD AGIN' HIM, AND THEN I KNOW SOMEBODY WHO'LL BACK HIM TWO TO ONE."

A PERTINENT QUESTION.

This cartoon faithfully reflected the sentiments of the Canadian people on the subject of annexation. While it is still true that there is no general feeling in favor of the change indicated, there is an appreciable absence of the unfriendly feeling toward the United States which was generally cherished at this time.

DIOGENES, JUNE 18th, 1869.

A PERTINENT QUESTION.

> MRS. BRITANNIA.—"IS IT POSSIBLE, MY DEAR, THAT YOU HAVE EVER GIVEN YOUR COUSIN JONATHAN ANY ENCOURAGEMENT?"
>
> MISS CANADA.—"ENCOURAGEMENT! CERTAINLY NOT, MAMMA. I HAVE TOLD HIM WE CAN *NEVER* BE UNITED."

"WELCOME THE COMING—SPEED THE PARTING."

About this time Hon. (now Sir) John Rose, late Minister of Finance in the Dominion Government, left Canada to take up his residence in England, where he still resides. Sir Alexander Galt, Mr. Rose's predecessor in the Finance Department, had recently re-entered public life. Both gentlemen had long been prominent citizens of Montreal.

DIOGENES, JULY 23rd, 1869.

"WELCOME THE COMING—SPEED THE PARTING!"

"FRIENDS IN COUNCIL;" OR, "IS THE GAME WORTH THE CANDLE?"

THE persons represented in this sketch are Hons. S. L. Tilley, Sir George Cartier and A. T. Galt. The latter gentleman resumed for a brief period the charge of the Finance Department, after the resignation of Hon. John Rose. The financial affairs of the new Dominion were not in the most prosperous condition at the moment.

DIOGENES, AUGUST 27th, 1869.

"FRIENDS IN COUNCIL;" OR, "IS THE GAME WORTH THE CANDLE?"

FORBIDDEN FRUIT.

Mr. L. S. Huntington, M.P. for Shefford (Quebec), had entered public life in 1861, and was chiefly distinguished for decided views in favor of Canadian Independence. He soon came to be looked upon as an annexationist in disguise—a fate which awaits every Canadian public man who avows Independence ideas. The Mr. Chamberlain in the cartoon was a gentleman of local repute.

DIOGENES, SEPTEMBER 24th, 1869.

FORBIDDEN FRUIT.

H—T—N.—"IT'S A VERY PRETTY PLUM—A VERY PRETTY PLUM, INDEED! ENOUGH TO MAKE ANYBODY'S MOUTH WATER!"

CH—MB—N.—"DON'T YOU WISH YOU MAY GET IT? THAT PLUM WILL TAKE SOME TIME TO RIPEN YET; AND WHEN IT FALLS, I FANCY 'OTHELLO'S OCCUPATION WILL BE GONE!'"

(SEE SPEECH OF MR. CHAMBERLIN AT THE BEDFORD AGRICULTURAL SHOW.)

UNCLE SAM KICKED OUT.

The anti-annexation sentiment which has always prevailed in Canada is presented with considerable "force" in this picture.

GRINCHUCKLE, SEPTEMBER 23rd, 1869.

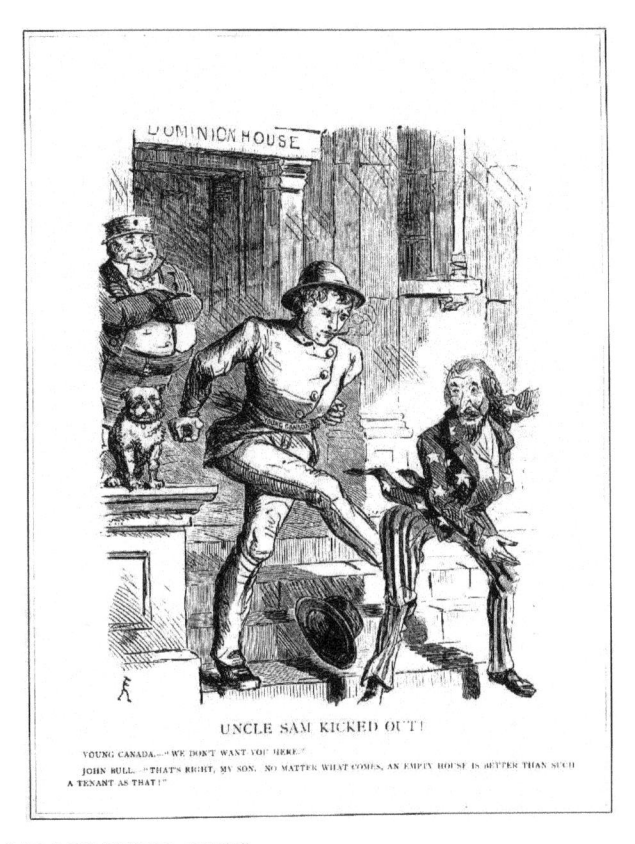

UNCLE SAM KICKED OUT!

YOUNG CANADA.—"WE DON'T WANT YOU HERE."

JOHN BULL.—"THAT'S RIGHT, MY SON. NO MATTER WHAT COMES, AN EMPTY HOUSE IS BETTER THAN SUCH A TENANT AS THAT!"

STIRRING TIMES AHEAD.

Hon. George Brown had been defeated in 1867 in South Ontario by Hon. T. N. Gibbs, and his place in Parliament as the leader of the Reform Party had remained vacant. It may be added that the "stirring times" anticipated in the cartoon were never realized so far as the House of Commons was concerned. On the accession of the Reform Government in 1873, Mr. Brown was offered and accepted a seat in the Senate.

GRINCHUCKLE, SEPTEMBER 30th, 1869.

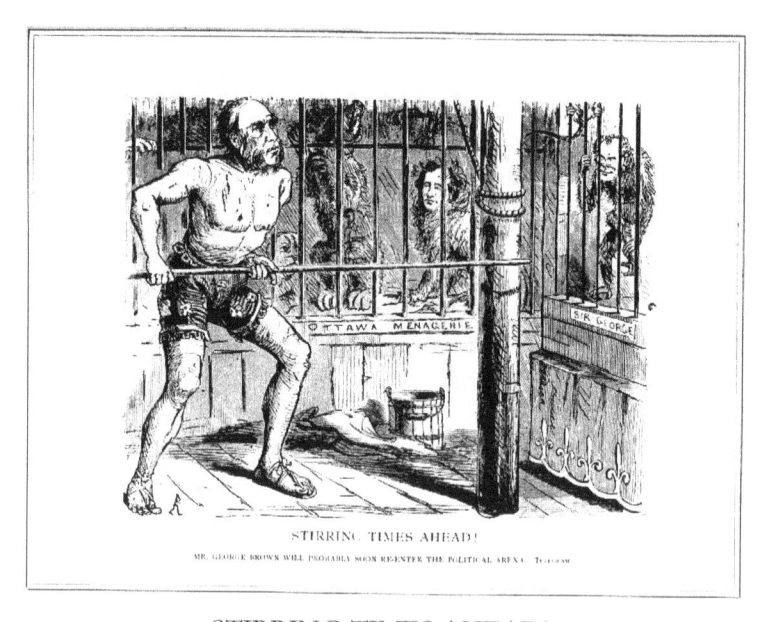

STIRRING TIMES AHEAD!

MR. GEORGE BROWN WILL PROBABLY SOON RE-ENTER THE POLITICAL ARENA.—TELEGRAM.]

TOO LATE!

This cartoon refers to the selection of Sir Francis Hincks for the post of Finance Minister, in opposition to the claims put forth by the press on behalf of others who were considered to be more entitled to the honor.

DIOGENES, OCTOBER 1st, 1869.

"TOO LATE."

FIRST OLD LADY.—"MY LITTLE BOY IS STRONG AND HEALTHY, AND—"

SECOND DITTO.—"MINE HAS BEEN PRACTISING FOR SOME TIME, AND IS QUITE FIT FOR THE PLACE."

MASTER JOHN.—"IT'S NO USE, MY GOOD WOMAN. THIS BOY THOROUGHLY UNDERSTANDS THE BUSINESS, AND KNOWS ALL THAT WILL BE REQUIRED OF HIM. I CAN'T DO ANYTHING

FOR YOU AT PRESENT, BUT I MAY SEND ONE OF YOUR LADS UP WEST BY-AND-BY."

THE POLITICAL "GIRL OF THE PERIOD."

In his speeches and writings, Mr. Huntington pictured Canadian Independence in glowing colors. This cartoon professes to show the "maiden" as she is.

DIOGENES, OCTOBER 15th, 1869.

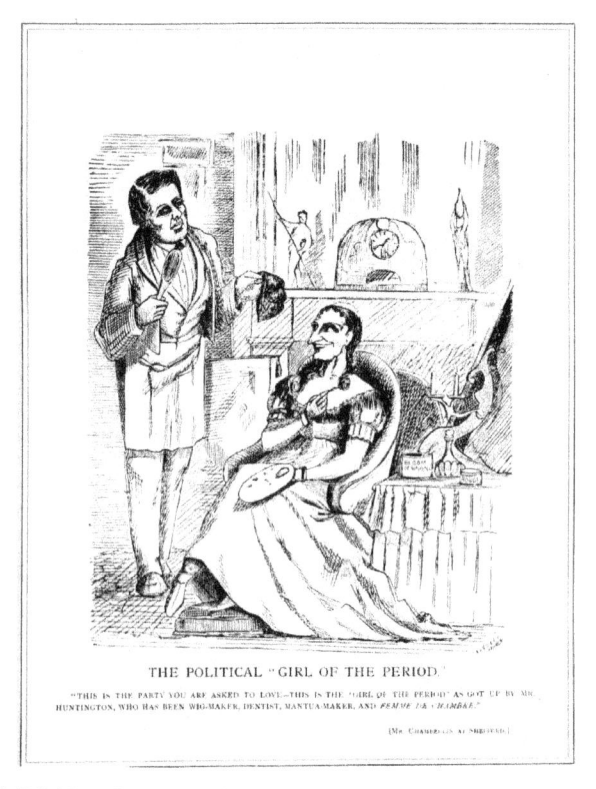

THE POLITICAL "GIRL OF THE PERIOD."

"THIS IS THE PARTY YOU ARE ASKED TO LOVE—THIS IS THE 'GIRL OF THE PERIOD' AS GOT UP BY MR. HUNTINGTON, WHO

HAS BEEN WIG-MAKER, DENTIST, MANTUA-MAKER, AND *FEMME DE CHAMBRE.*"

MR. CHAMBERLIN AT SHEFFORD.

"L'HOMME QUI RIT."

Upon accepting office as Finance Minister in the Dominion Cabinet, Sir Francis Hincks presented himself for election in the constituency of Renfrew, the sitting member, Mr. Rankin, making way for him. Sir Francis had declared that the acceptance of office at this time involved personal sacrifice on his part.

DIOGENES, OCTOBER 22nd, 1869.

"L'HOMME QUI RIT."

—L'astre d'un favori,

Qui se croyait un grand ministre,

Quand de nos maux il avait ri.

—*Béranger.*

SCENE FROM THE COMEDY OF "THE TICKET-OF-LEAVE MAN."

Sir Francis Hincks had but shortly returned to Canada from the Windward Islands, where he had for several years occupied the position of Governor. The claim that he was making a "personal sacrifice" in accepting office seems to have been too much for *Diogenes*.

DIOGENES, OCTOBER 29th, 1869.

THE COMEDY OF "THE TICKET-OF-LEAVE MAN."

(Adapted to the Ottawa stage.)

MISS CANADA.—"YOU'LL TAKE CARE OF THE MONEY, WON'T YOU? YOU KNOW I'M NOT VERY RICH."

MR. MELTER MOSH.—"O, YESH, MA TEAR, I'LL LOOK AFTER TE MONISH! I'M A HONEST MAN; IF YOU DON'T BELIEVE ME, AX BARBADOES AND DEMARARA. DEY KNOW ME, TEN YEARS."

A MOONLIGHT SCENE ON THE OTTAWA.

This is another reference to the selection of Sir Francis Hincks as Finance Minister in preference to the other available candidates for the position.

GRINCHUCKLE, NOVEMBER 4th, 1869.

A MOONLIGHT SCENE ON THE OTTAWA.

GRINCHUCKLE.—"FAITH! IF HE GETS AT IT, THERE WILL BE VERY LITTLE LEFT FOR KING CROW OR ANYONE ELSE."

KING CROW.—"IF SOME OF THESE NORTH RENFREW MEN WOULD ONLY FRIGHTEN HIM AWAY NOW, WOULDN'T THE LIKE OF ME HAVE OUR FILL!"

FROM HALIFAX TO VANCOUVER.

The project of an all rail route from the Atlantic to the Pacific on Canadian territory had begun to be agitated. The incredulity attributed to Uncle Sam in the cartoon was fully shared by many more immediately interested. The year 1886, however, saw the feat accomplished.

DIOGENES, NOVEMBER 5th, 1869.

FROM HALIFAX TO VANCOUVER.

MISS CANADA.—"THIS IS WHAT WE WANT, COUSIN JONATHAN. IT WILL GIVE US REAL INDEPENDENCE, AND STOP THE FOOLISH TALK ABOUT ANNEXATION."

JONATHAN.—"WAL, MISS, I GUESS YOU'RE ABOUT RIGHT THAR; BUT I'LL BELIEVE IT WHEN I SEE IT."

WAITING FOR THE CAT TO JUMP.

This cartoon gives an intimation that the views of Mr. Luther H. Holton on the subject of Canada's future destiny were not perfectly clear and fixed. In this Mr. Holton was by no means singular among our public men. The insinuation that he was a blind follower of public opinion does him less than justice.

GRINCHUCKLE, NOVEMBER 18th, 1869.

WAITING FOR THE CAT TO JUMP!

MR. HOLTON.—"DRAT THE CAT! I CAN'T DO ANYTHING TILL I SEE HOW SHE JUMPS!"

THE DOMINION CURTIUS.

Another ironical allusion to Sir Francis Hincks' vast "personal sacrifice" in accepting the emoluments of office. The allusion is to the classic story of

Curtius saving Rome by jumping into the chasm. The attendant heroes are Honorable George Brown and Sir John Macdonald.

DIOGENES, NOVEMBER 19th, 1869.

THE DOMINION CURTIUS.

MACDOUGALL'S SOLILOQUY.

Hon. William Macdougall was appointed to the Lieut.-Governorship of the North-West Territories on the cession of that country to the Dominion by the Hudson Bay Co. The Half-breed settlers, however, deeming it an infringement of their rights that the country was ceded without their formal consent, opposed Mr. Macdougall's entrance on his arrival. He was obliged to return without enjoying the office he had gone to assume.

GRINCHUCKLE, NOVEMBER 25th, 1869.

MACDOUGALL'S SOLILOQUY.

"THERE IS NOT MUCH FUN IN THIS GAME, BUT A MOVE MUST BE MADE WHEN THE KING IS IN CHECK."

"HOPE TOLD A FLATTERING TALE."

Sir Narcisse Fortunat Belleau, Lieutenant-Governor of Quebec, is the principal figure in this cartoon. The financial position of the Province was not satisfactory at this time, and the hope expressed in the speech from the throne, to which allusion is made, was one which the people would cordially share.

GRINCHUCKLE, DECEMBER 2nd, 1869.

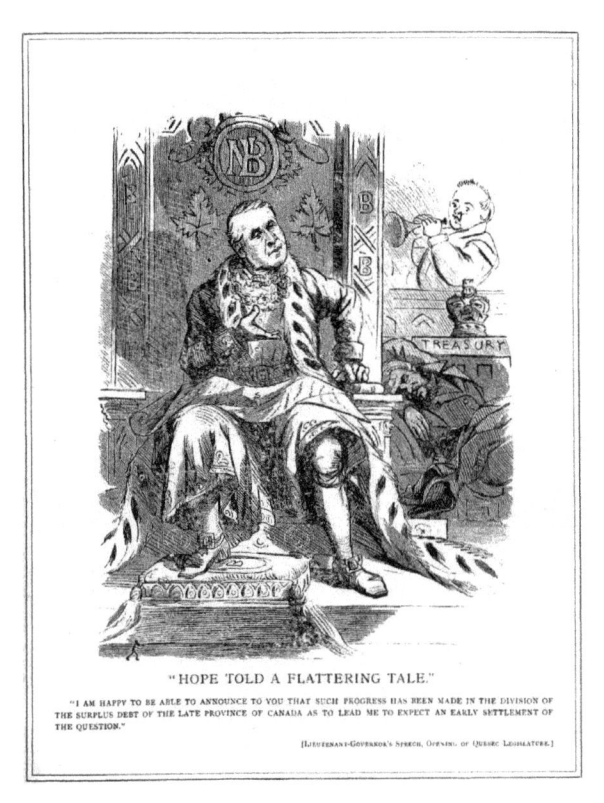

"HOPE TOLD A FLATTERING TALE."

"I AM HAPPY TO BE ABLE TO ANNOUNCE TO YOU THAT SUCH PROGRESS HAS BEEN MADE IN THE DIVISION OF THE SURPLUS DEBT OF THE LATE PROVINCE OF CANADA AS TO LEAD ME TO EXPECT AN EARLY SETTLEMENT OF THE QUESTION."

LIEUTENANT-GOVERNOR'S SPEECH, OPENING OF QUEBEC LEGISLATURE.

ENOUGH IS AS GOOD AS A FEAST.

This was an allusion to the debate which took place on the Nova Scotia "better terms" resolution in the House of Commons. Mr. Blake introduced a motion setting forth the unconstitutionality of the bargain which had been made after the Act of Union, under which Nova Scotia got additional subsidy. Honorable J. S. Macdonald, on the other hand, supported the action of the Government. In connection with this cartoon *Grinchuckle* addressed the following lines to "Joe Howe":—

It's of no use, Joe Howe, to be craving for plunder,

For we know you are but a political rake;

And Ontario will never consent to strike under,

While she has for her leader redoubtable Blake.

Old Sandfield, we know, is a premier squeezable,

And he's willing to give, and you're eager to take;

He would buy up your Province by any means feasible;

But he cannot buy up that redoubtable Blake.

GRINCHUCKLE, DECEMBER 9th, 1869.

ENOUGH IS AS GOOD AS A FEAST.

J. S. McD———LD.—"YES, MY PET, YOU SHALL HAVE IT. I COULD NOT FIND IT IN MY HEART TO DEPRIVE YOU OF IT."

E. BL———E.—"YOUR PET! SHE WAS NOT ALWAYS SO; BUT IF YOU DARE, I'LL TEAR THE LOLLY-POPS FROM YOUR MEDDLING HAND."

THE CANADIAN BARNUM NOW EXHIBITING AT QUEBEC.

The "Court" of Lieutenant-Governor Belleau was conducted in a style of magnificence quite out of harmony with the democratic spirit of the people, as well as the condition of the Provincial purse. This grandeur, with its ridiculous accompaniments of "state balls," etc., was encouraged by Sir Geo. Cartier, whose own tastes were courtly. The subject offered too tempting a theme to escape caricature.

GRINCHUCKLE, JANUARY 6th, 1870.

THE CANADIAN BARNUM NOW EXHIBITING AT QUEBEC.

C—RT—R.—"HERE YOU SEE DE LEETLE CREATURES PERFORMING SOME OF DERE AMUSING—WHAT YOU CALL IT?—FEATS."

EXTREMES MEET.

The Half-breeds of Manitoba were in rebellion under the leadership of Louis Riel, on account of their alleged rights having been ignored in the bargain with the Hudson Bay Company. They demanded compensation for the land assumed by the Dominion. The artist cites this as a parallel to the position assumed by Mr. Howe on behalf of Nova Scotia, when "better terms" were demanded, and secured.

GRINCHUCKLE, JANUARY 27th, 1870.

EXTREMES MEET.

JOE (FROM THE EAST).—"GO IT! BE A PATRIOT; AND YOU'LL SELL WELL,—LIKE ME."

LOUIS (IN THE WEST).—"YOU'RE AN UNPRINCIPLED OLD SCAMP; BUT IF I DON'T GET MY $5000 A YEAR, BLOW ME TIGHT."

THE YOUNG LADY'S APPEAL TO A "GALLANT KNIGHT."

Sir Francis Hincks was the author of the Canadian "Shinplaster" currency, a scheme adopted to drive out the American silver. The cartoon will be understood from the following legend which accompanied it:—

MISS CANADA: O, Sir Francis, I am suffering so much from this light American silver skate. It is no mate for the heavy gold one on my other foot. The doctors differ, but I shall never get along without another gold one.

SIR FRANCIS H———S: The doctors be fiddled! Who asked the doctors? I'm your doctor! You shall have the gold skate, my dear. Mr. Weir will attend to it. Meantime you can strengthen your ankle with a twenty-five cent Dominion plaster.

MISS CANADA: A thousand thanks. Oh, I'm so glad! (Aside: *But I'll burn the Plaster!*)

SIR FRANCIS H———S (whose hearing is sharp): I hope you will?

GRINCHUCKLE, FEBRUARY 10th, 1870.

THE YOUNG LADY'S APPEAL TO A "GALLANT KNIGHT."

THE MID-DAY GUN AT OTTAWA.

This cartoon is chiefly interesting as giving amusing portraits of a number of prominent parliamentarians. It is the custom to fire a gun from Nepean Point, opposite the House of Parliament, at twelve o'clock, noon, each day, which gives distinguished personages and others an opportunity of regulating their watches. At the date of this cartoon, workmen were engaged in making some additions to the central block.

CANADIAN ILLUSTRATED NEWS, MAY 11th, 1872.

THE MID-DAY GUN AT OTTAWA.

JOHN CANUCK'S NEW ROAD.

Great dissatisfaction was expressed in the Maritime Provinces at the rejection of the St. John Valley route for the Intercolonial Railway. The change to the route subsequently selected—a much longer and costlier one—was made as the result of a conference with the Imperial authorities by Sir F. Hincks and Hon. Mr. Chandler, of New Brunswick. The contemplated expense of the road was a matter of serious concern, however, to all the Provinces.

CANADIAN ILLUSTRATED NEWS, MAY 11th, 1872.

JOHN CANUCK'S NEW ROAD.

MR. JOHN K. NUCKE (*a gentleman farmer*).—"A fine balance at my banker's, eh! Glad to hear it! What's the next improvement you intend carrying out? For I've noticed a surplus always indicates some grand scheme concocted between you and the hands on the farm. Now tell me; out with it!"

STEWARD.—"Well, Your Honour ought to have a road made to the lake; it would open up your property, and keep the hands busy, and——"

MR. J. K. N.—"Well, well! and what will it cost?"

STEWARD.—"Oh! a mere trifle; some thirty millions or so; and if that don't pay the contractor we will give him some of our waste land, you know. We might spare 40 or 50 million acres and never feel it!"

MR. J. K. N.—"Whew! (*whistle*). Hem! Ho, ho! Well, we'll talk over it."

SCENE FROM THE MERRY WIVES OF WINDSOR.

An allusion to the annexation utterances of Hon. Joseph Howe. The figures in the group are Sir George E. Cartier, Sir John Macdonald, Sir Francis Hincks, and Mr. H. L. Langevin.

CANADIAN ILLUSTRATED NEWS, MARCH 30th, 1872.

SCENE FROM "THE MERRY WIVES OF WINDSOR."

SHALLOW.—"I HAVE LIVED FOUR-SCORE YEARS AND UPWARDS; I NEVER HEARD A MAN OF HIS PLACE, GRAVITY, AND LEARNING, SO WIDE OF HIS OWN RESPECT."—ACT III., SCENE I.

THE GAME OF SEE-SAW.

The Maritime Provinces exhibited much fickleness in the bestowal of their political favor. In the first general election after Confederation only one supporter of the Conservative ministry was returned. In the next election, this state of affairs was exactly reversed.

CANADIAN ILLUSTRATED NEWS, MAY 4th, 1872.

A GAME OF SEE-SAW.

SKETCHES FROM THE CAPITAL.

"TOODLES" AT TORONTO.

Mr. Rykert, a prominent member of the Opposition in Ontario, had taken a prominent part in the attack made upon the Government for extravagant expenditure in the furniture and fittings of the apartment occupied by Hon. A. McKellar, Minister of Agriculture.

CANADIAN ILLUSTRATED NEWS, MARCH 29th, 1873.

"TOODLES," AS PERFORMED AT THE PROVINCIAL HALL, TORONTO, ON THE 13TH INST.

MRS. TOODLES. (HON. A——D MCK——R.)—But, my dear Toodles.

TOODLES. (MR. R——T.)—Oh, don't dear Toodles me—you'll drive me mad—your conduct is scandalous in the extreme.

MRS. T.—My dear Toodles, don't say so.

TOODLES.—But I will say so, Mrs. Toodles. What will become of us, with your passion for "contingencies." I say, Mrs. Toodles, where's the money, and echo answers, where.

MRS. T.—I'm sure, my dear Toodles, I lay it out to the best advantage.

TOODLES.—You shall not squander and waste our revenue.

MRS. T.—My dear, I buy nothing but what is useful.

TOODLES.—Use*ful*—use*less* you mean. I won't have the house turned into a museum for glass-ware and chromos. At the end of the year I ask, where's the money—all gone too—spent in infernal nonsense.

THE MANY-COUNSELLED ULYSSES.

This was one of a series of sketches by Mr. E. Jump, in which he cleverly dressed leading Canadian politicians in the costumes and characters of classic heroes. The aptness of the delineation in this case will be recognized by all.

CANADIAN ILLUSTRATED NEWS, APRIL 12th, 1873.

THE MANY-COUNSELLED ULYSSES.

THE MANY-COUNSELLED ULYSSES.

"Ulysses, first in public cares, she found,

For prudent counsels like the gods renowned."

[POPE, *Iliad II.*, 205, 6.]

"AFTER THE SESSION."

On the 2nd of April, 1873, Honorable L. S. Huntington, member for Shefford, from his place in the House, charged Sir John A. Macdonald with having corruptly sold to Sir Hugh Allan the charter of the proposed Canadian Pacific Railway, for a large sum of money, which had been used as a Ministerial Bribery Fund in the preceding General Election. Shortly after this, and before any decided enquiry had been made into the matter, Parliament was adjourned (on May 23rd) until the following 13th of August. The cartoon playfully suggests the feeling of the Opposition, represented by Hon. A. Mackenzie, towards the accused Ministry during the "vacation."

GRIP, MAY 31st, 1873.

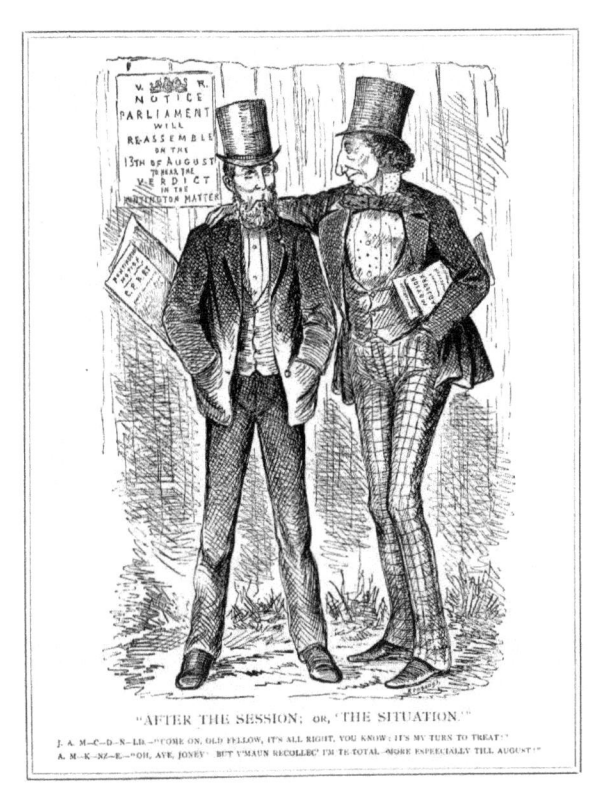

"AFTER THE SESSION; OR, 'THE SITUATION.'"

J. A. M—C—D—N—LD.—"COME ON, OLD FELLOW, IT'S ALL RIGHT, YOU KNOW; IT'S MY TURN TO TREAT!"

A. M—K—NZ—E.—"OH, AYE, JONEY! BUT Y'MAUN RECOLLEC' I'M TE-TOTAL—MORE ESPEECIALLY TILL AUGUST!"

"CANADA'S LAOCOON."

An adaptation of the classical story of Laocoon and the serpents to the circumstances of some of the parties to what was already known as the "Pacific Scandal." The persons represented are Sir Hugh Allan, (to whom the charter was sold), Sir John Macdonald, and Sir Francis Hincks. It is due to the latter gentleman to point out that, as indicated in the cartoon, he was merely *suspected* of complicity in the matter, and most emphatically denied the truth of the allegation of his guilt, made in some of the newspapers.

GRIP, JULY 19th, 1873.

"CANADA'S LAOCOON;"

OR, VIRGIL ON THE POLITICAL SITUATION.

"Ecce autem gemini a Tenedo, tranquilla per alta, &c."—ÆNEID, BOOK II.

(*Freely Translated.*)

"When lo! two snakes (perhaps from the Yankee shore),

Together trail their folds across the floor,

With precious scandals reared in front they wind,

Charge after charge, in long drawn length behind!
While opposition benches cheer the while,
And JOHN A. smiles a very ghastly smile!—and—"
Everybody knows the rest!

"WILL HE COME TO GRIEF?"

The legend of this cartoon sufficiently explains its import. The facetious occupation of the Clown had its analogue in the course pursued by the *Globe* during the "Scandal" excitement—an eager desire to see the hero of the business unseated.

GRIP, JULY 26th, 1873.

WILL HE COME TO GRIEF?

THE THRILLING ACT NOW IN THE RING OF THE POLITICAL CIRCUS.

"DUFFERIN'S TORMENTORS."

The Ministerial party in the House, headed by Sir John Macdonald, were exceedingly anxious for a prorogation of Parliament,—the Opposition as earnestly opposed that course. Their counter entreaties to the Governor-General on the subject suggested the familiar scene of the railway passenger and his friends the "cabbies."

GRIP, AUGUST 2nd, 1873.

"DUFFERIN'S TORMENTORS, OR *PER VIAS RECTAS.*"

J—N A. (ANXIOUSLY).—"CARRIAGE, SIR? 'MINISTERIAL' HOTEL— ONLY CONSTITUTIONAL PLACE IN THE CITY—COME ALONG WITH ME, SIR."

Mc—K—NZ—(EAGERLY).—"THIS WAY, MY LORD—'REFORM' HOUSE! TAK' THE RIGHT COURSE—GIE' US YER CHECKS!!"

L—D D—FF—N.—"MUCH OBLIGED, GENTLEMEN, I ASSURE YOU; BUT I HAVE A 'RIG' OF MY OWN AT HAND, YOU KNOW."

"THE DAINTY DISH."

A note here is perhaps superfluous. The faces of the "blackbirds" in the "pie" are those of Hon. M. Langevin, (a prominent member of the Macdonald Government), Sir Hugh Allan, James Beaty, Esq., (to represent the *Leader*), Sir John A. Macdonald, Sir Francis Hincks, "Uncle Sam," and T. C. Patteson, Esq., (representing the *Mail* newspaper). On Messrs. Blake and Mackenzie devolved the task of presenting the savory dish before Parliament.

GRIP, AUGUST 9th, 1873.

"ISN'T THAT A DAINTY DISH TO SET BEFORE A KING?"—
NURSERY RHYME.

"WHITHER ARE WE DRIFTING."

General indignation was expressed throughout the country, when, in accordance with the advice of the implicated Premier, Parliament was prorogued, and the investigation of the scandal thus delayed. The words imputed to Sir John in the cartoon had been used by him on the floor of the House, and became a popular by-word while the discussion on the subject lasted.

GRIP, AUGUST 16th, 1873.

WHITHER ARE WE DRIFTING?

"THE BEAUTIES OF A ROYAL COMMISSION."

This cartoon was intended to satirize the appointment by Sir John A. Macdonald of a Royal Commission, composed of his own friends, to inquire into and report upon the charges brought by the Hon. Mr. Huntington. The sentiment of the press and public with regard to this proceeding justified the implication of the caricature, that the accused Premier was virtually "trying himself."

GRIP, AUGUST 23rd, 1873.

THE BEAUTIES OF A ROYAL COMMISSION.

"WHEN SHALL WE THREE MEET AGAIN?"

"WAITING FOR HUNTINGTON."

Hon. Mr. Huntington refused to acknowledge the Royal Commission appointed by the accused Minister, and declined to submit his case before it. The motive imputed to him by the Conservative press for this refusal was fear, and in the eyes of his friends Sir John sustained the attitude represented in the cartoon.

GRIP, AUGUST 30th, 1873.

WAITING FOR HUNTINGTON!

"THE IRREPRESSIBLE SHOWMAN."

Apropos of the visit to Canada of Barnum, the Showman, during the Pacific Scandal "fever."

GRIP, SEPTEMBER 13th, 1873.

THE IRREPRESSIBLE SHOWMAN.

BARNUM WANTS TO BUY THE "PACIFIC SCANDAL."

"BLACKWASH AND WHITEWASH."

"Illustrating," as the legend goes on to say, "the recent great Opposition speeches, and the doings of the jolly Royal Commission." The Reformers, of course, lost no opportunity of painting Sir John in grimy colors; while it was generally acknowledged that the Royal Commissioners and the Conservative press did little more during the excitement than "whitewash" him.

GRIP, SEPTEMBER 20th, 1873.

BLACKWASH AND WHITEWASH.

ILLUSTRATING THE RECENT GREAT OPPOSITION SPEECHES, AND THE DOINGS OF THE JOLLY ROYAL COMMISSION.

"WE IN CANADA SEEM TO HAVE LOST ALL IDEA OF JUSTICE, HONOR AND INTEGRITY."

So said the *Mail*, the leading Conservative organ, on September 26th. GRIP sought to point this lugubrious confession with an illustration drawn from the topic of the hour.

GRIP, SEPTEMBER 27th, 1873.

"WE IN CANADA SEEM TO HAVE LOST ALL IDEA OF JUSTICE, HONOR AND INTEGRITY."—THE MAIL, 26TH SEPTEMBER.

"PROGRESSING FAVORABLY."

A peep into the hearts of the Reform leaders during the interesting period of Sir John Macdonald's political "indisposition." The "Poor dear Premier" may be seen, if **the reader** will take the trouble to **peer** into the bedroom.

GRIP, OCTOBER 4th, 1873.

"PROGRESSING FAVORABLY."

MISS CANADA (Anxiously).—"DOCTORS, HOW DO YOU FIND THE POOR DEAR PREMIER?"

DR. B—N (For the M.D.'s).—"MADAM, WE'VE JUST HAD A CONSULTATION; THE SYMPTOMS ARE HOPEFUL—WE BELIEVE HE CAN'T SURVIVE OCTOBER!"

"REHEARSING FOR THE 23RD."

Representing the spirit in which the Leaders of the respective parties approached what was expected to be the decisive date.

Grip, October 11th, 1873.

REHEARSING FOR THE 23RD INSTANT.

M—K—ZIE—"I WILL FIGHT HIM UPON THIS THEME UNTIL MY EYELIDS WILL NO LONGER WAG!"—Hamlet, Act v., Scene 1.

JOHN A.—"WHAT DO I FEAR?"—Richard III., Act v., Scene 3.

"WILL HE GET THROUGH?"

The question which was on all lips during the interim between the prorogation of the House of Commons on the 13th of August and the day fixed for its re-assembling, October 23rd. The prophecy conveyed in the unreasonable smallness of the hoop in the clown's hand was duly realized.

Grip, October 18th, 1873.

"WILL HE GET THROUGH?"

"A CASE OF RIEL DISTRESS."

The murder of Thomas Scott, at Fort Garry, during the Red River Rebellion, naturally excited great indignation throughout the Dominion, and a universal demand was made for the apprehension and punishment of Louis Riel, the leader of the malcontents, at whose instigation the deed was committed. This righteous sentiment, however, ultimately resolved itself into mere political "claptrap," the Conservative Government, then in power, having secretly promised the rebels an amnesty, while publicly professing an anxious desire to "catch him."

GRIP, OCTOBER 25th, 1873.

A CASE OF *RIEL* DISTRESS!

"Of comfort no man speak;

Let's talk of graves, of worms, and epitaphs!"—SHAKESPEARE.

Typical of the overwhelming grief which seized the Conservative party on being turned out of office, after a reign of nearly twenty years.

GRIP, NOVEMBER 1st, 1873.

"OF COMFORT NO MAN SPEAK;
LET'S TALK OF GRAVES, OF WORMS, AND EPITAPHS!"—
Shakespeare.

"MISS CANADA'S SCHOOL."

Being a word of advice to the new Premier. The persons represented in the Cartoon are, commencing at the head of the "class," Hon. A. Mackenzie, Hon. Edward Blake, Hon. George Brown, Hon. E. B. Wood, Louis Riel (who had been elected M.P. for Provencher, Manitoba), Hon. M. Langevin, James Beaty, Esq., M.P., T. C. Patteson, Esq., manager of the *Mail*, Sir Francis Hincks, and Sir John Macdonald. Monitor, His Excellency, Earl Dufferin, Governor-General.

Grip, November 8th, 1873.

MISS CANADA'S SCHOOL (DEDICATED TO THE NEW PREMIER).

MISS CANADA (TO THE BOY AT THE HEAD)—"NOW, ALEXANDER, BE VERY CAREFUL, OR I'LL PUT YOU WHERE JOHN IS!"

"THE POLITICAL MOTHER HUBBARD."

It had been currently reported in the newspapers that the dignity of the Lieut.-Governorship of Ontario was to have been bestowed on the Hon. George Brown, immediately on the accession to power of the Reform Government. The new Ministers discovered, however, that Sir John Macdonald had, in the last gasp of his official life, appointed one of his own colleagues (the Hon. John Crawford) to the position in question, besides disposing of ninety-nine other "places" in the gift of the First Minister.

GRIP, NOVEMBER 15th, 1873.

THE POLITICAL MOTHER HUBBARD

AND JOHN A.'S "DYING INIQUITY."

"THE IRREPRESSIBLE JACK."

The circumstances under which Sir John Macdonald was deposed from power seemed to warrant the assumption of the Reformers that he was "done for." But, on the contrary, it only seemed the signal for additional honors to be heaped upon him by the Conservative Party, who unhesitatingly chose him leader of the Opposition, and nominated him as member for Kingston, West Toronto, etc., not to mention banquets, and other species of emphasis.

GRIP, NOVEMBER 22nd, 1873.

THE IRREPRESSIBLE JACK; OR, THE CONSERVATIVE RESUSCITATION.

JOHN A. (SIDE SHOWMAN)—"DID YOU THINK THE LITTLE FELLER'S SPRING WAS BROKE, MY DEARS?"

"THE PREMIER'S MODEL."

In an address to the electors of Lambton, soon after the accession to power of the Reform Party, Mr. Mackenzie declared the cardinal points of the Policy he would inaugurate, as leader, to be "Electoral Purity" and "the Independence of Parliament." (Before entering political life, Mr. Mackenzie followed the vocation of stone-mason.)

GRIP, NOVEMBER 29th, 1873.

THE PREMIER'S MODEL;
OR, "IMPLEMENTS TO THOSE WHO CAN USE THEM."

Canada—"WELL AND BRAVELY DONE, MACKENZIE; NOW STAND BY THAT POLICY, AND I'M WITH YOU ALWAYS!"

"THE POLITICAL GIANT-KILLER."

The "Canada First" movement, having for its object the cultivation of a national sentiment and the extinction of political party strife, was inaugurated about this time.

Grip, December 13th, 1873.

THE POLITICAL GIANT-KILLER; OR, "CANADA FIRST."

"THE WEST TORONTO RUN."

In the General Election which followed the defeat of the Conservative Government, Mr. E. O. Bickford contested West Toronto in the interest of the New Opposition, and rested his claims to the seat mainly on the prestige of Sir John Macdonald, declaring that, if elected, he would follow that honorable gentleman through weal or woe. As the cartoon suggests, he met with defeat.

GRIP, DECEMBER 20th, 1873.

THE WEST TORONTO RUN.

B—CKF—RD (Jockey of the Nag "John A.")—"SAY, GOV'NOR, LOOK HERE, THIS HOSS AIN'T WO'TH SHUCKS ON HIS OWN MERITS!"

"CHRISTMAS PIE."

The treat which Santa Claus had in store for the Reformers.

Grip, December 27th, 1873.

"CHRISTMAS PIE."

JOHNNY'S "TURN;" OR, NEW YEAR'S JOY.

The election of Mr. D'Arcy Boulton as Conservative member for South Simcoe, in the Ontario Legislature, took place about this time. Although the influence of this event on the fortunes of the late Premier of the Dominion was hardly discoverable, it was hailed by the Conservative press as the earnest of a reaction in favor of that party. A Mr. Saunders (whose face our artist had not seen) was Mr. Boulton's opponent in the contest.

GRIP, JANUARY 3rd, 1874.

JOHNNY'S "TURN," OR NEW YEAR'S JOY.

"THE CRUEL OBJECT OF DISSOLUTION."

Mr. Mackenzie and his colleagues advised the dissolution of Parliament on taking office. This was accordingly carried out, with the object, as the cartoon suggests, of keeping Sir John and his comrades "out in the cold."

GRIP, JANUARY 10th, 1874.

THE CRUEL OBJECT OF "DISSOLUTION."

THE CRUEL OBJECT OF "DISSOLUTION."

"POLITICAL PASTIMES."

Political sport, analogous to this, occupied the minds of the "boys" and the newspapers during the recess.

GRIP, JANUARY 31st, 1874.

POLITICAL PASTIMES.

"PITY THE DOMINIE; OR, JOHNNY'S RETURN."

Anent the re-election of Sir John A. Macdonald as member for Kingston, in the general election which followed the accession of the Reform Government.

GRIP, FEBRUARY 7th, 1874.

PITY THE DOMINIE; OR, JOHNNY'S RETURN.

CANADA—"HERE'S OUR JOHNNY FOR YOU AGAIN, MR. MACKENZIE! YOU'LL FIND HIM APT ENOUGH, BUT FRANKLY, SIR, HE'S FULL OF MISCHIEF!"

"THE NEW DEPARTURE."

Hon. Edward Blake's withdrawal from the new Government, very shortly after it had taken possession of the Treasury Benches, created an unpleasant sensation throughout the country. The hon. gentleman had been perhaps the main instrument in bringing about a fall of the preceding Cabinet.

GRIP, FEBRUARY 21st, 1874.

THE NEW DEPARTURE.

Spouse B———e.—"FAREWELL FOR THE PRESENT, DEAR; YOU AND THE GIRLS MUST MANAGE THE HOUSE IN MY ABSENCE!"

"THE CURSE OF CANADA."

Whiskey.
Grip, February 28th, 1874.

THE CURSE OF CANADA.

IS THERE NO ARM TO SAVE?

"THE OPPOSITION QUARTETTE."

The most prominent members of the Opposition (Conservative) in the Ontario Legislature were Messrs. M. C. Cameron, Q.C., J. Chas. Rykert, A. W. Lauder and A. Boultbee. These gentlemen were always most active and energetic in their labor of fault-finding, and at the time of the cartoon were ringing the changes on the public accounts of the Province, which were undergoing examination in Committee.

GRIP, MARCH 7th, 1874.

THE OPPOSITION QUARTETTE.

PERFORMING THE NEW AND HIGHLY AGGRAVATING AIR ENTITLED "PUBLIC ACCOUNTS."

"A QUESTION FOR PAY DAY."

The "Opposition Quartette" had vigorously assailed the action of the Hon. A. McKellar for having, in his capacity as Minister of Public Works, granted a half holiday (at the public expense) to the workmen engaged in building the Central Prison at Toronto, to allow them an opportunity of attending a nomination meeting in the West Division of the city. In view of the meagre amount of work done on the left side of the Speaker during the session, GRIP'S question was quite logical.

GRIP, MARCH 21st, 1874.

A QUESTION FOR PAY DAY; OR, "CENTRAL PRISON" LOGIC APPLIED.

GRIP (LOQ.)—"GENTLEMEN, IS THERE ANY 'SCANDAL' ABOUT YOUR DRAWING A FULL SESSION'S PAY FOR NO WORK AT ALL?"

"'GRIP'S' PERPETUAL COMEDY."

The adjournment of the Ontario Legislature was immediately followed by the assembling of the Dominion Parliament at Ottawa.

GRIP, MARCH 28th, 1874.

"GRIP'S" PERPETUAL COMEDY.

"THEY HAVE THEIR EXITS AND THEIR ENTRANCES."

"THE VACANT CHAIR."

Louis Riel, the leader of the Red River Rebellion and alleged murderer of Thomas Scott, had been returned for Provencher, Manitoba, to the Dominion Parliament. He prudently failed to take his seat in the House, while the unanimity with which both sides cried for his arrest made "the vacant chair" a bond of union for the time being.

GRIP, APRIL 4th, 1874.

THE VACANT CHAIR.

A *RIEL* BOND OF UNION.

"THE SCIENCE OF CHEEK."

A great sensation was caused throughout the country at the announcement that Riel had actually appeared in the House at Ottawa and signed the Members' Roll. This he did *incog.*, and immediately afterwards disappeared. The cartoon anticipated his next step in the "Science of Cheek."

GRIP, APRIL 11th, 1874.

THE SCIENCE OF CHEEK; OR, RIEL'S NEXT MOVE.

RIEL (LOQ.)—"FIVE TOUSSAND DOLLARS! BY GAR, I SHALL ARREST ZE SCOUNDREL MYSELF!"

"A TOUCHING APPEAL."

On the accession of Mr. Mackenzie's Government a large deficit in the treasury was discovered. Mr. (now Sir Richard) Cartwright, Finance Minister, in his Budget speech, attributed this to the extravagance and corruption of the preceding Administration. A new tariff was issued, in which the duties on various articles were raised considerably.

GRIP, APRIL 18th, 1874.

A TOUCHING APPEAL.

("TOUCHING" THE SECRET OF INCREASED TAXATION.)

YOUNG CANADA—"SAY, UNCLE JOHN, WON'T YOU GIVE ME A 'DEFICIT?' MA SAYS YOU GAVE THE GRITS ONE!"

"MRS. GAMP'S HOME-THRUST."

Early in the session a committee was appointed to inquire into the cause of the North-West difficulties, and during the progress of the inquiry evidence was elicited (mainly from Archbishop Tache) which implicated Sir John A. Macdonald. The Reform Party is represented in the cartoon as facetiously anticipating a repetition of the right hon. gentleman's famous asseveration of his innocence.

GRIP, MAY 2nd, 1874.

MRS. GAMP'S HOME-THRUST.

SAIREY GAMP (The Reform Party).—"'AVEN'T GOT NOTHINK TO SAY ABOUT THEM 'ANDS THIS TIME, I SUPPOGE, MISTER SIR JOHN?"

"PACIFIC PASTIMES."

The Reform Government took up the Pacific Railway scheme, but initiated a new policy with regard to it. Sir John Macdonald had pledged the country to complete the entire work within ten years. Mr. Mackenzie characterized this as a physical impossibility, and proposed, as the cartoon has it, "to tak' the distance in sensible like jumps, ye ken!"

GRIP, MAY 16th, 1874.

PACIFIC PASTIMES; OR, THE HARD "ROAD TO TRAVEL."

"DIGNITY" WITHOUT "IMPUDENCE."

The Dominion Senate, usually so passive and quiet, strikingly signalized its life and vim during this session by throwing out a bill introduced by Mr. Cameron, M.P. for South Huron, having for its object the re-distribution of the electoral divisions composing that Riding.

GRIP, MAY 23rd, 1874.

"DIGNITY" WITHOUT "IMPUDENCE."

OLD MADAME SENATE—"I SAY, MR. LOWER-HOUSE MACKENZIE, WHO'S RUNNING THIS COUNTRY, ANYHOW?"

JUSTICE AND GENEROSITY

Hon. (now Sir) A. A. Dorion, a prominent leader of the Rouge or French Reform Party, occupied the office of Minister of Justice in the Government of Hon. Alexander Mackenzie. In this capacity he offered to himself in the capacity of an able lawyer, a seat upon the Bench of his Province, which offer was gratefully accepted. He still occupies the position (1886).

GRIP, JULY 6th, 1874.

JUSTICE & GENEROSITY; OR, "HOIST WITH HIS OWN"—
PREROGATIVE.

MRS. MINISTER OF JUSTICE DORION (TO THE HON. A. A.
DITTO)—"HE WAS A GOOD 'ITTLE GRITTSY-TITTSY, SO HE
WAS, AND HE SHALL HAVE A NICE 'ITTLE SOFT SEATSY-
TEETSY, SO HE SHALL!"

ST. GEORGE AND THE DRAGON

As an outcome of reckless malice, amidst the passionate decisions of politics about this time, one of the Conservative papers published a scandalous libel reflecting upon the Hon. George Brown's private character. With characteristic promptitude the assailed gentleman had the paper indicted, and a full apology was made. To those who knew Mr. Brown, there was no need of his trouble in this matter, but the event served as an illustration of his uncompromising self-respect.

GRIP, AUGUST 8th, 1874.

"SAINT GEORGE AND THE DRAGON."

"SAINT GEORGE AND THE DRAGON."

THE CHIEF MOURNERS

An ingenious romancer on the staff of the *Mail*, had, some months before this, concocted a "scandal" at the expense of Hon. Archibald McKellar, a member of the Ontario Cabinet. The story—which was regarded from the first as a joke—was to the effect that Mr. McKellar had purchased for his official apartment a portrait of an unknown lady. This imputation of gallantry to the bucolic Minister—a man in all respects the reverse of the ideal knight—was what constituted the "point." The alleged picture soon took its place in the armory of the Opposition and was constantly referred to as that

- 135 -

of "Little Mrs. Blank." In the Public Accounts Committee about the date of our cartoon, explanations were made by Messrs. Ewing & Co., from whom certain pictures had been purchased, which completely killed this pleasant fiction, and "Little Mrs. Blank" was no more. The leading Members of the Opposition—Messrs. M. C. Cameron, A. Boultbee, C. J. Rykert and A. W. Lauder—were supposed by the artist to have been much cast-down at the sudden demise of such a valuable auxiliary.

GRIP, SEPTEMBER 12th, 1874.

THE CHIEF MOURNERS.

THE PLAIN FACT

The amended election law (introduced by the government of Mr. Mackenzie) was purposely made very stringent as a measure against bribery and corruption, and at this time trials were first conducted under its provisions. It so happened that the first victims were members of the party that had passed the measure, but the slaughter was by no means confined to that party. The expression "Come along, John, and put down bribery and corruption" had been imputed to a supporter of one of the unseated members, in the course of the election trial of Col. Walker, the member elect, at London, and for a considerable time the phrase was one of the catch-words of the Conservative Party.

GRIP, SEPTEMBER 19th, 1874.

THE PLAIN FACT.

MACKENZIE—"COME ALONG, JOHN, AND PUT DOWN
BRIBERY AND CORRUPTION; NEITHER OF US CAN RIDE VON
MULE YET AWHILE."

THE PROFESSOR'S "BRIDAL" FOR PARTYISM

In the columns of the *Canadian Monthly* and the *Nation* (a weekly paper devoted to "Canada First" ideas), Prof. Goldwin Smith had written eloquently against the system of party government, more especially in the Provincial Houses. He advocated a fusion of the parties on the ground that there were no questions of principle to divide them. Mr. Brown, in the *Globe*,

- 138 -

strongly opposed the theory, as a matter of course. Mr. William H. Howland was the originator of the Canada First Party, and a warm friend of Prof. Goldwin Smith.

GRIP, OCTOBER 10th, 1874.

THE PROFESSOR'S "BRIDAL" FOR PARTYISM; OR, THE DREAM OF "CURRENT EVENTS."

SEE THE CANADIAN MONTHLY FOR OCTOBER.

SIGNOR BLAKE IN HIS CELEBRATED ACT OF KEEPING THE *GLOBE* IN SUSPENSE

Mr. Blake had made what the *Globe* called a "disturbing speech" at Aurora, in which he expressed some advanced ideas, and referred rather vaguely to the existence of a Reform Party that could find nothing to reform. As Mr. Blake was regarded as a man whose whole-hearted support was all but essential to the success of the Reform Ministry then in office, the attitude he occupied was most unsatisfactory to the chief Government organ. Mr. Goldwin Smith and Mr. Howland, as representatives of the Canada First Party, fancied they could detect some gleams of hope for that propagander in Mr. Blake's speech.

GRIP, OCTOBER 31st, 1874.

SIGNOR BLAKE IN HIS POPULAR ACT OF KEEPING THE *GLOBE* IN SUSPENSE.

THE NEW CONSERVATIVE

By way of indirect reproof to Mr. Blake for his "disturbing" speech, and, perhaps, with special reference to that gentleman's implied stricture on a "Reform party with nothing to Reform," the *Globe* expressed its disapproval of the spirit of restless change, and intimated that there were times when Reformers could "rest and be thankful" without losing their right to the name. The Conservative party in the Ontario House were, at the time, in sore need of recruits; and, no doubt, would have welcomed the accession of this new Conservative.

GRIP, NOVEMBER 7th, 1874.

THE NEW CONSERVATIVE.

SEE THE GLOBE, WEDNESDAY, NOV. 4.

SIX AND HALF A DOZEN

As a reply to the jibes of the *Globe* on the subject of political corruption, the Conservative party recalled the record of Mr. George Brown in the Brown *vs.* Gibbs contest in South Ontario, some years previously. This election, it was alleged, had been characterized by glaring instances of bribery on the Reform side; but there was, in those days, little or no legal restraint put upon such tactics.

GRIP, NOVEMBER 28th, 1874.

SIX AND HALF A DOZEN.

SIR JOHN—"MR. BROWN, DO YOU THINK YOU COULD GO THROUGH THIS HOOP AS WELL AS I WENT THROUGH THAT ONE, IF YOU HAD A 'TRIAL'"?

CHRISTMAS MORNING

In accordance with the time-honored custom, Mr. Grip fills the stockings of his *proteges* with good things, in recognition of Christmas, which comes "but once a year."

GRIP, DECEMBER 26th, 1874.

CHRISTMAS MORNING; OR, THE POLITICAL STOCKINGS.

POLITICAL PLUCK

This widely-known chromo was adapted to the situation of the Ontario Opposition without the necessity for any change in the figures. Messrs. Cameron, Rykert and Boultbee, as the acknowledged leaders of the Conservatives in the Local House, maintained a constant allegiance to their Federal leader, Sir John Macdonald, both in and out of the local arena. It was a well-known fact that amongst that astute politician's most eager desires, was a longing to get possession of the treasury benches of Ontario, upon which a Reform Government had long been firmly seated.

GRIP, JANUARY 16th, 1875.

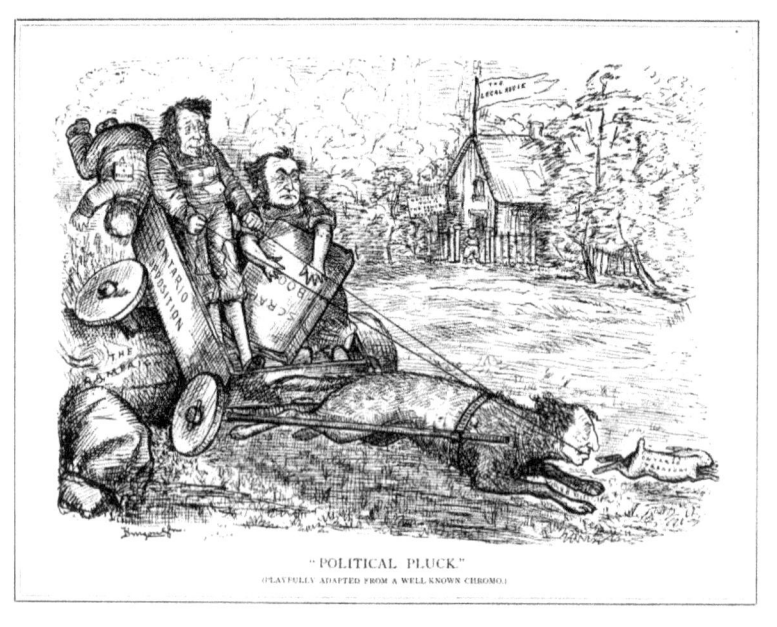

"POLITICAL PLUCK."

(PLAYFULLY ADAPTED FROM A WELL-KNOWN CHROMO.)

THE POLITICAL INTELLIGENCE OFFICE

Hon. Adam Crooks, Minister of Education in the Mowat Cabinet, having been defeated in East Toronto, remained for some months without a seat in the House. Hon. William Macdougall, who had been politically "everything by turns and nothing long," and who had failed to get a Lieutenant-Governorship in Manitoba, or a seat in East York, was at this time showing a disposition to throw in his lot with the Reform Party, but met with small encouragement.

GRIP, JANUARY 30th, 1875.

THE POLITICAL INTELLIGENCE OFFICE; OR, SITUATIONS WANTED.

LOYALTY IN A QUANDARY

In the House of Commons, Sir John Macdonald sought to make a point against the Mackenzie Government for having declared an amnesty to those concerned in the Half-breed rebellion in Manitoba, which amnesty included Lepine, one of the rebel leaders, who had been condemned to death. As, at this time, the prerogative of clemency was vested in the Crown, the action to which exception was taken was that of the Governor-General and not of the Government. By the efforts of Hon. Edward Blake, a change was subsequently made in the Governor-General's instructions, by which the responsibility in this, as in other matters, was vested in the Government.

GRIP, FEBRUARY 6th, 1875.

LOYALTY IN A QUANDARY; OR, THE "LEPINE CASE" MADE PLAIN.

OTHELLO BROWN'S APOLOGY

Hon. George Brown had undertaken a mission to Washington, on behalf of the Government, to secure a reciprocity treaty between the United States and Canada, but was unsuccessful in his efforts. Mr. Brown was now a prominent member of the Canadian Senate.

GRIP, FEBRUARY 27th, 1875.

OTHELLO BROWN'S APOLOGY,

BEFORE THE SENATE, FEBRUARY 15TH, 1875.

WAITING FOR THE SIGNAL

The growing sentiment of the country against the liquor traffic had been voiced in Parliament by Mr. G. W. Ross, a member of the Reform Party. The Government expressed a willingness to consider the subject of Legal Prohibition as soon as they had evidence that a majority of the people desired such a measure. Rev. Mr. Afflick, an eloquent English lecturer, was at this time making a tour of Canada in the interest of the temperance cause.

GRIP, MARCH 6th, 1875.

WAITING FOR THE SIGNAL.

ARTEMUS WARD MILLS AND BETSY JANE SENATE

Hon. David Mills, Minister of the Interior in the Mackenzie Government, had moved a resolution in the House looking to the reorganization of the Dominion Senate. By the Confederation Act, the Members of the Senate were appointed for life, by the Governor in Council. A Conservative Ministry having made most of the appointments the Chamber naturally partook of a complexion highly unsatisfactory to the Liberal Party.

GRIP, MARCH 13th, 1875.

ARTEMUS WARD MILLS AND BETSY JANE SENATE.

THE NERVOUS PASSENGER

The *Globe* looked upon Mr. Mills' anti-Senate agitation with disfavor perhaps because Hon. George Brown had assented to the appointive principle as a member of the Government which drew up the Constitutional Act. It has already been noted that Mr. Blake's Aurora speech had "disturbed" the Liberal organ, and that Mr. Goldwin Smith's theories were also regarded as dangerous in that quarter. Under this combination of circumstances Mr. Brown's Conservative tendencies were severely jolted.

GRIP, MARCH 20th, 1875.

THE NERVOUS PASSENGER.

THE POLITICAL SPELLING-SCHOOL

The popular craze at this date was "Spelling Matches." The persons represented in the cartoon were prominent members of the respective parties; those on the left (Conservative) being: Sir John A. Macdonald, Hon. M. C. Cameron, Messrs. P. Mitchell, Beatty, Patteson, Bunster, Alonzo Wright and Rykert; on the right (Reform) Messrs. Brown, Blake, Mackenzie, Laird, McKellar and Mowat, with Mr. Goldwin Smith. Mr. Samuel Platt, M.P., for East Toronto, had just passed successfully through the ordeal of an election trial, and is commended for his correct spelling of "Purity," a word which had often bothered some of the other boys.

GRIP, MAY 1st, 1875.

GRIP'S POLITICAL SPELLING MATCH.

A GUESS AT THE GREAT SLEEPER'S DREAM

Mr. Blake had on several occasions spoken in favor of Imperial Federation— a scheme under which the colonies would send representatives to the Home Parliament. Taken in connection with the known fact that public life in Canada was but little to the taste of the able gentleman, GRIP ventured to conjecture that a seat in the Imperial House, with its broader arena, might be amongst the visions of his moments of reflection.

GRIP, MAY 15th, 1875.

A GUESS AT THE GREAT SLEEPER'S VISION.

RE-ORGANIZING THE QUARTETTE

Hon. William Macdougall, at that time a Member of the Ontario Assembly, was regarded as an opponent of the Government. His ability assured for him a prominent position, and Mr. C. J. Rykert having obtained a seat in the House of Commons, Mr. Macdougall was supposed to have taken his place as a member of the celebrated "Quartette." The cartoon represents the members as tuning up for a performance.

GRIP, MAY 22nd, 1875.

RE-ORGANIZING THE QUARTETTE.

WILLIAM McD—G—LL (New Recruit)—"I'M PERFECTLY IN ACCORD WITH MR. CAMERON."

MR. DAVENPORT BLAKE IS PUT INTO THE CABINET

Mr. Blake was induced to accept a seat in the Mackenzie Ministry without portfolio. His presence added a great element of strength to the Government, but the gratification of his colleagues at his accession was somewhat modified by the fear that he might at any moment begin to play upon the "disturbing" instruments.

Grip, May 29th, 1875.

MR. DAVENPORT BLAKE IS PUT INTO THE CABINET.

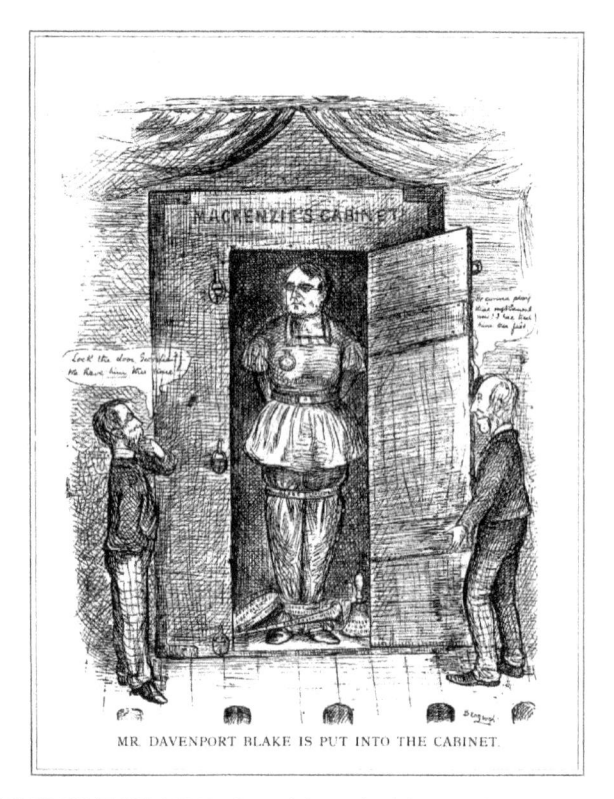

MR. DAVENPORT BLAKE IS PUT INTO THE CABINET.

PERFECT FREEDOM! O, FOR LIBERTY!

Mr. Mackenzie was at this time on a visit to his native country, where he was honored with the freedom of Perth and Dundee, and otherwise handsomely recognized. It had long been a common saying in Canada that Mr. George Brown, through the *Globe*, exercised a supreme influence over the Reform Government.

GRIP, JULY 24th, 1875.

PERFECT FREEDOM! O, FOR LIBERTY!

THE POLITICAL SITUATION

Mr. Goldwin Smith's teachings on the subject of "No Partyism" excited the hostility of both Grit and Tory partizans, and his position between the *Globe* and *Mail* was precisely that of the hapless school-boy pictured in the chromo of which the cartoon is an adaptation.

GRIP, JULY 31st, 1875.

THE POLITICAL SITUATION.

(ADAPTED FROM A POPULAR CHROMO.)

THE UNPATRONIZED NOSTRUM VENDOR

The note to Cartoon No. 120 might be repeated as a comment upon this. Mr. Smith was the recipient of a good deal of violent abuse in reply to his attacks on Partyism, and being naturally a man of uncommon sensitiveness, and very impatient of criticism, his lot was indeed "not a happy one."

GRIP, AUGUST 7th, 1875.

THE UNPATRONIZED NOSTRUM VENDOR.

PROFESSOR SMITH'S SERMON ON PARTYISM

It is needless to say to those who know anything of Mr. Goldwin Smith that he defended himself against his critics with passionate brilliancy. The sentence he is represented as speaking in the cartoon occurred in one of his retorts upon the *Globe*, and was considered unusually cutting as an exposition of that journal's strict religious orthodoxy in contrast with its merciless treatment of its opponents.

GRIP, AUGUST 21st, 1875.

PROFESSOR SMITH'S SERMON ON ATHEISM.

(SEE THE "NATION," AUGUST 13TH.)

INCONSISTENT PRACTICE OF FREE TRADE DR. BROWN

Mr. George Brown was an earnest advocate of the Free Trade principle in political economy, and was always vigorous in his denunciation of the opposite principle in any direction. About this time the *Globe* had earnestly denounced the action of the Ontario Society of Physicians and Surgeons for having prosecuted an unlicensed practitioner, under a law which the *Globe* always regarded as narrow and tyrannical. This was not very consistent with the attitude it sustained towards Mr. Goldwin Smith as a healer of the body politic. Mr. Alderman Baxter, well-known in Toronto, is used as a metaphorical figure of Justice.

GRIP, SEPTEMBER 4th, 1875.

INCONSISTENT "PRACTICE" OF FREE TRADE DR. BROWN.

PISTOLS FOR THREE

Rev. Egerton Ryerson, D.D., was drawn into the Brown-Smith controversy, and it soon became what is known as a "game of cut-throat"—each against the others. GRIP, believing that, in the stereotyped newspaper phrase, "this correspondence had gone on long enough," was tempted to suggest a fatal shot all round as perhaps the only way of securing a "rest" for the reading public.

GRIP, SEPTEMBER 11th, 1875.

PISTOLS FOR THREE; OR, THE TRIANGULAR "DUEL."

CANADIAN POLITICS: A PICTURE FOR THE PARTIES

Mr. Goldwin Smith continued his attacks upon Partyism with unabated vigor in the columns of the *Nation* and the *Canadian Monthly*, his contention being that the chief end and aim of both "factions" was office.

GRIP, SEPTEMBER 25th, 1875.

CANADIAN POLITICS: A PICTURE FOR THE "PARTIES."

POLITICAL PURITY; OR, POT AND KETTLE

Mr. George Brown had written a letter to a political friend—Senator Simpson—asking for a contribution towards the election fund of the Reform Party in the heat of the general election. This letter was secured by the Conservative Party, and commented upon as a set-off to the celebrated telegram of Sir John Macdonald, calling upon Sir Hugh Allan for "another $10,000." Mr. Brown vigorously denied that he had used any of the money contributed for other than legitimate expenses, or that his letter had been written with any corrupt intent.

GRIP, OCTOBER 2nd, 1875.

POLITICAL PURITY; OR, POT AND KETTLE.

THE MINISTERIAL SHANTY

Mr. Joseph Cauchon, a prominent representative of Quebec, was taken into the Mackenzie Cabinet. M. Cauchon had, some time previously, been denounced by Mr. Brown, in connection with an episode in his Provincial career, as a most unworthy man. The incident referred to—that of making a speculation at the expense of the inmates of the Beauport Asylum at Quebec—was characterized by Mr. Brown as an offence that was "rank and smelled to heaven," and this expression was constantly quoted by the Tory press during M. Cauchon's connection with the Ministry.

GRIP, DECEMBER 18th, 1875.

THE MINISTERIAL SHANTY; OR, THE CAUCHON AT HOME.

THE EQUIVOCAL RECOMMEND

The note to No. 127 will sufficiently explain the difficulty the *Globe* found in giving M. Cauchon a very hearty "send off" as Member of the Reform Administration.

GRIP, DECEMBER 25th, 1875.

THE EQUIVOCAL RECOMMEND.

"IF THE *GLOBE* BELIEVES M. CAUCHON FIT TO SIT IN THE MINISTRY, IT OWES HIM AN APOLOGY FOR MALIGNING HIM IN THE PAST."—*KINGSTON WHIG*.

THE PRINCE OF ORANGE

Hon. Mackenzie Bowell occupied a high place in the Conservative ranks by virtue of his connection with the Orange Order; Sir Hector Langevin was regarded as similarly representing Ultramontane views. Politically and personally they were warm friends and colleagues. The cartoon was a satirical allusion to some Orange "bounce" that had been indulged in by Mr. Bowell out of the House.

GRIP, FEBRUARY 19th, 1876.

THE "PRINCE OF ORANGE;" OR, ANYTHING TO BEAT THE GOVERNMENT.

RUNNING BEFORE THE PROTECTION WIND

The Conservative Party, becoming weary of the cold shades of opposition, took advantage of the "hard times" to proclaim a policy of Protection to Home Industries as the only salvation for the country. The Government, it was alleged, was largely responsible for the depression, and could relieve it only by raising the tariff. This cry seemed to meet with popular approval.

GRIP, MARCH 18th, 1876.

RUNNING BEFORE THE PROTECTION WIND.

THE POLITICAL SAMSON

Mr. Blake had settled down into a steady and efficient Member of the Administration, though the popular belief was that his heart was not really in his toil.

GRIP, MARCH 25th, 1876.

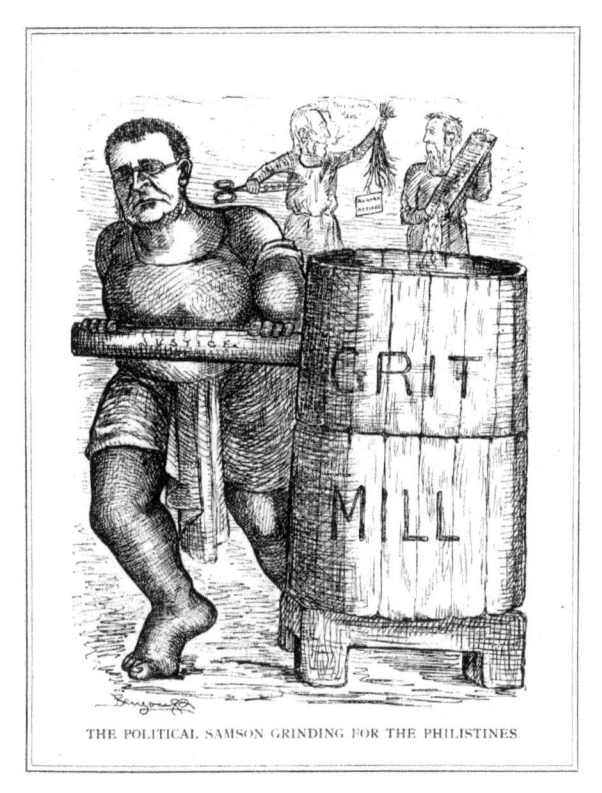

THE POLITICAL SAMSON GRINDING FOR THE PHILISTINES.

EATING THE LEEK; OR, "HENRY V." AS LATELY PLAYED IN THE COMMONS

Mr. Mackenzie had been charged with nepotism in connection with the purchase of steel rails for the C. P. R.—the contract for the purchase having been awarded to a firm in which it was alleged the Premier's brother had an interest. This charge had been repeated frequently upon the hustings, although Mr. Mackenzie had demonstrated that it was unfounded. His explanation upon the floor of Parliament at this time gave the final death blow to the slander.

GRIP, APRIL 8th, 1876.

EATING THE LEEK;

OR, "HENRY V." AS LATELY PLAYED IN THE COMMONS.

FLUELLAN.—MR. MACKENZIE. — PISTOL.—DR. TUPPER.

THE DEPRESSION COMMITTEE SIMPLIFIED

The Protection agitation induced the Government to appoint a committee to investigate the causes of the Depression of Trade. This committee was composed mainly of Government supporters, well-known to be free-traders, and its report was to the effect that a Protective Tariff would not cure the difficulty, which arose from causes beyond Governmental control.

GRIP, APRIL 29th, 1876.

THE "DEPRESSION COMMITTEE" SIMPLIFIED.

THE "DEPRESSION COMMITTEE" SIMPLIFIED.

OFF WITH HIS HEAD

The Crooks Act, a measure intended to further restrict the evils of the liquor traffic, came into force at this time. Under the provisions of this Act the number of licenses to be issued by any municipality was limited, and the consequence was a wholesale "decapitation" of liquor sellers throughout the Province. The Act was framed by Hon. Adam Crooks, and in the cartoon is being appropriately carried out by Hon. O. Mowat, the head of the "Executive."

GRIP, MAY 6th, 1876.

OFF WITH HIS HEAD!

"RICHARD III.," AS PLAYED BY MR. CROOKS THROUGHOUT THE PROVINCE.

THE COOL RECEPTION

Sir A. T. Galt, a statesman to whom reference is frequently made in earlier sections of this work, felt called upon to lift a warning voice against the political pretentions of the Romish hierarchy in Canada. With this view he delivered an able lecture on "Church and State" in Toronto. His effort met with considerable popular applause but was studiously ignored by the newspaper organs of both the political parties, plainly out of regard to "the Catholic vote."

GRIP, JUNE 10th, 1876.

THE COOL RECEPTION.

G. B. AND JOHN A.—"SORRY WE CAN'T RECEIVE YOU CORDIALLY, MR. GALT; BUT—YOU SEE HOW IT IS."

MASTER OF THE SITUATION

Mr. Justice Wilson, speaking from the Bench in the matter of Simpson vs. Wilkinson (a suit for libel which arose out of the publication of a letter from Hon. George Brown to Senator John Simpson, requesting a contribution to the Reform Election Fund), declared emphatically that the letter had been written for corrupt purposes. This Mr. Brown had repeatedly denied, offering to account for the expenditure of every cent contributed to the fund in question. The Judge's repetition of the statement—which Mr. Brown contended had been actuated by political malice—threw the *Globe* into great fury, and the learned jurist was "handled without gloves" in several articles.

GRIP, JULY 15th, 1876.

MASTER OF THE SITUATION.

TRYING TO SMUGGLE ACROSS

Sir John Macdonald had so far recovered his self-assurance by this time, that he and his followers were calmly asserting that there really was "nothing in" the Pacific Scandal. The Conservative press had in fact ceased to call it a "Scandal" at all; "Slander" was the word now used. The possibility that Sir John could so far regain the confidence of the Canadian people as to get back to office was amongst the things the *Globe* regarded as ridiculous.

GRIP, JULY 29th, 1876.

TRYING TO SMUGGLE ACROSS.

POLICEMAN G. B.—"NOTHING IN IT! THEN WHY NOT VINDICATE YOURSELF BY HAVING IT THOROUGHLY EXAMINED."

THE POLITICAL MRS. SQUEERS

To the upright and respectable members of the Conservative Party the Pacific Scandal had been a terrible blow, and amongst these there was none whose character stood higher than that of Hon. M. C. Cameron, the leader of the Opposition in the Ontario Assembly. The exigencies of his position, however, made it imperative that he should be in accord with the Party at large, and in due course he brought himself to believe that there was more *slander* than *scandal* in the unpleasant affair.

GRIP, AUGUST 5th, 1876.

THE POLITICAL MRS. SQUEERS AND HER NAUSEOUS DOSE.

THE ONLY SATISFYING PICNIC AFTER ALL

While the Reformers were enjoying the good things of office, Sir John and his principal colleagues were passing the summer in making a picnic tour. The political picnic had become of late years a Canadian institution, and although there were pleasures to be derived from the outings in the leafy woods, with their accompanying buns, lemonade and political addresses, these were not to be compared to the attractions of the Treasury Benches.

GRIP, AUGUST 19th, 1876.

THE ONLY SATISFYING PICNIC, AFTER ALL!

BRANDED

The *Mail* proved a most vigorous and alert Oppositionist and lost no opportunity for an attack upon the Government, whether fair or foul. For the sake of political capital it did not hesitate to "run down" the country, and thus to furnish the European press with arguments against emigration to Canada. The incident which called forth the cartoon was the *Mail's* endorsation of a baseless slander on Canada which had been forwarded to the London *Times* from California.

GRIP, SEPTEMBER 2nd, 1876.

BRANDED!

FOR ENDORSING UNFOUNDED SLANDERS AGAINST CANADA.

DETECTED

During the Session of Parliament it was discovered that Mr. Anglin, Speaker of the House of Commons, and proprietor of the *St. John Freeman*, had, during the recess, performed $8,000 worth of "extra printing" for the Government. This, being contrary to the spirit and letter of the Independence of Parliament Act, created a strong feeling against the Cabinet. The *Globe*, greatly at a loss to find an excuse for the job, suggested that Mr. Mackenzie had given the work to his supporter "inadvertently."

GRIP, SEPTEMBER 9th, 1876.

DETECTED.

G. B. (THE INNOCENT PAGE.)—"PLEASE, MR. POLICEMAN, I KNOW IT ISN'T RIGHT, BUT PERHAPS MR. MACKENZIE GAVE IT TO HIM INADVERTENTLY."

FALSTAFF AND HIS FOLLOWERS

In a speech at Watford, Mr. Mackenzie had stated that one of the "hon. gentlemen" who were then on a tour with Sir John Macdonald, had been the first to apply to the Reform Government for an appointment. The reference was well understood to be to Hon. William Macdougall.

GRIP, SEPTEMBER 16th, 1876.

FALSTAFF AND HIS FOLLOWERS.

SIR JOHN A. FALSTAFF.—"IS THIS TRUE, PISTOL?"—MERRY WIVES OF WINDSOR, ACT I., SCENE 1.

CONFEDERATION, THE MUCH-FATHERED YOUNGSTER

Although the historical facts as to the origin of the idea of Confederation were familiar to most intelligent Canadians, (and they by no means the oldest inhabitants,) there was a standing dispute as to the party to whom the honor of its paternity belonged. Claims were put forth (amongst others,) on behalf of Messrs. George Brown, Sir F. Hincks, Wm. Macdougall and Sir John A. Macdonald.

GRIP, SEPTEMBER 30th, 1876.

CONFEDERATION!

THE MUCH-FATHERED YOUNGSTER.

THE TRANSPARENT FACTS

His Excellency the Governor-General (Lord Dufferin) undertook a mission to British Columbia, in connection with a vice-regal visit, to bring about, if possible, a good understanding between that Province and the Dominion on the subject of the projected Canada Pacific Railway. The British Columbians were at the moment in a state of great excitement over what they regarded as a breach of faith by the Federal Government, and were even threatening secession. Lord Dufferin was, as usual, successful in his efforts at peace-making. The "transparent facts" given in the cartoon detail the various stages of the difficulty up to the date of Lord Dufferin's intervention.

GRIP, OCTOBER 7th, 1876.

THE TRANSPARENT FACTS.

IN THE MATTER OF THE "CARNARVON TERMS."

THE NEW CABINET MINISTER

Mr. David Mills (to whom reference has been made in cartoon No. 113), was now taken into the Cabinet as Minister of the Interior, to the evident dissatisfaction of the *Globe*, which regarded him as dangerously radical in his views on the Senate and other questions. As has already been noted, Mr. Blake was also looked upon as a young man rather inclined to be "fast." On the appointment of Mr. Mills, the *Mail* expressed a sympathy for Mr. Mackenzie which was very touching under the circumstances.

GRIP, OCTOBER 27th, 1876.

THE NEW CABINET MINISTER.

LITTLE BOY MACKENZIE PICKS UP MORE "FAST" COMPANY.

THE POLITICAL COLONEL SELLERS

The character of *Colonel Sellers* as presented by Mr. John T. Raymond, in the comedy of "The Gilded Age," was at this time the rage in dramatic circles. The *Colonel* was an amusingly imaginative speculator, who, though enduring abject penury, was "in his mind" revelling in luxury. Being obliged by cruel fortune to restrict his diet to cold water and raw turnips, he rose equal to the occasion and gave it out that these staples were his special choice as table delicacies. Being unable to afford fuel for his stove, he used a lighted candle therein, on the philosophical ground that it was not heat but merely the *appearance* of heat that was required. This eccentric genius found a political anti-type in Sir John, who was now bravely making the best of his reversed circumstances.

GRIP, NOVEMBER 11th, 1876.

THE POLITICAL "COLONEL SELLERS."

THE CONSERVATIVE POSITION

That the adoption of the Protective Policy was a mere piece of political tactics on the part of the Conservative leader was demonstrated in every move from first to last. He and his chief supporters in Parliament had been throughout their whole public career adherents of the revenue-tariff system equally with their opponents, and it was asking too much of public credulity to require the people to believe that they had been soundly converted to Protectionism in a moment, and that moment just before a general election when there was wide-spread grumbling at the hard times.

GRIP, DECEMBER 2nd, 1876.

THE CONSERVATIVE POSITION.

PADDY MACDONALD.—"BEGORRA, I DON'T CARE FWITCH IT'LL TAKE ME TO, AV IT ONLY TAKES ME TO ME OWLD PLACE AT OTTAWAY."

NOT GUILTY, BUT DON'T DO IT AGAIN

Hon. George Brown having been cited to appear for contempt of court in connection with his strictures on Mr. Justice Wilson, (see cartoon 136) pleaded justification and argued his own case. The Judges before whom the proceedings were held having disagreed, the matter was allowed to drop.

GRIP, JANUARY 6th, 1877.

"NOT GUILTY," BUT DON'T DO IT AGAIN!

GEORGE BROWN'S LAWYER GIVES HIM A BIT OF ADVICE, GRATIS.

ORANGE BILL CROSSING THE POLITICAL BOYNE

Demands had been made upon the Ontario Government for a Special Act incorporating the Orange Society. The Government steadily resisted the appeal on the ground that such an Act would be class-legislation, and that the demand was made, not in good faith, but for the purpose of embarrassing the Reform Party in the interests of their opponents, with whom the Orange leaders were allied. At length, however, the *Globe* came out in favor of the Act, and urged the Government to grant the demand and end the difficulty. This advice the Ministry disregarded through the influence, it was generally believed, of Hon. C. F. Fraser, the able Roman Catholic Member of the Cabinet. Subsequently a General Act was passed, under which any organization of a legitimate character could secure incorporation.

GRIP, FEBRUARY 10th, 1877.

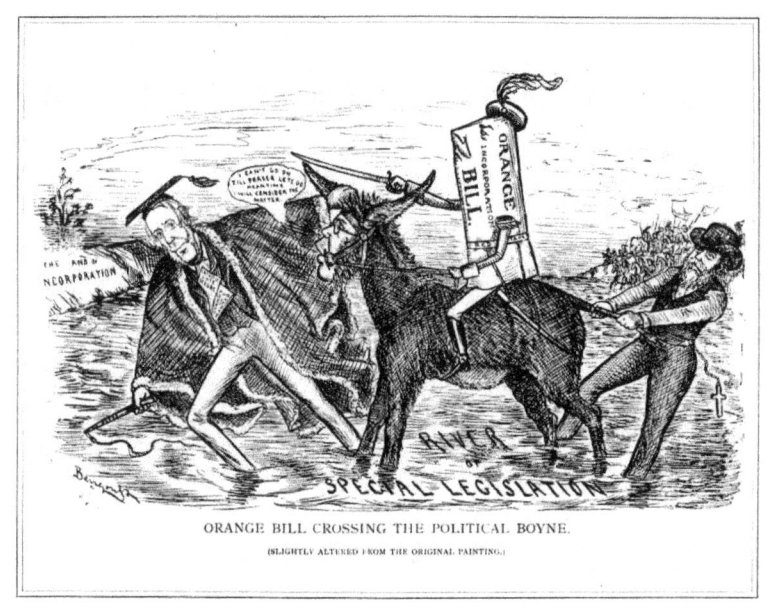

ORANGE BILL CROSSING THE POLITICAL BOYNE.

(SLIGHTLY ALTERED FROM THE ORIGINAL PAINTING.)

NOT A REAL LION.

At the numerous political picnics throughout the country, Sir John and his lieutenants were loud in their denunciations of the Government in connection with various scandals. In the presence of their opponents in Parliament, however, they refrained from formulating their charges or pressing for investigation.

Grip, February 17th, 1877.

NOT A REAL LION—EXCEPT OUTSIDE THE HOUSE.

John A.—

"You ladies, you, whose gentle hearts do fear ...

When lion rough in wildest rage doth roar, (at picnics, etc.)

Then know that I, one 'John the Trickster,' am

A lion's fell nor else no lion's dam."—*Midsummer Night's Dream.*

THE SIGNS OF THE ZODIAC GOING BACK ON VENNOR

Mr. Vennor, a civil engineer of Montreal, had become widely celebrated as a weather prophet, on the strength of a rather remarkable record of successful predictions. His forecast for February, 1877, however, was utterly astray, and a great deal of ridicule was indulged in at his expense.

Grip, March 10th, 1877.

THE SIGNS OF THE ZODIAC GOING BACK ON VENNOR.

THE BLUE GLASS CURE

Just at this time the craze for *blue glass* as a medium for the "healing rays" of the sun, was at its height. Marvellous cures by this agency were reported from various quarters—generally a considerable distance away. The claims put forward by the Conservatives as to the virtues of *protection* to cure the commercial depression, were very much like those of the blue glass specialists.

GRIP, MARCH 17th, 1877.

THE "BLUE GLASS" CURE FOR THE SICK CHILD.

THE SECRET SERVICE DEPARTMENT

After the accession to power of the Mackenzie Government it was found that a balance to the credit of the secret service fund had been chequed out of the Bank of Montreal by Sir John A. Macdonald, although that gentleman was no longer in an official position. Sir John declined to make any explanation of the matter on the ground that the disposition of secret service money was a matter that no one had a right to enquire into. The affair gave rise to a great deal of discussion, but, although Sir John's position was generally regarded as unsound, no official action was taken in the matter.

GRIP, MARCH 31st, 1877.

THE NEW "GOVERNMENT DEPARTMENT,"

AND THE SELF-APPOINTED MINISTER.

WHAT INVESTIGATION REVEALED

During the Session of Parliament some startling facts were made known as to the relations of the Northern Railway Company to the late Government. The Company was deeply indebted to the Dominion, and had been making vigorous efforts to get the amount reduced. For the purpose of influencing favorable legislation to this end, it was found that large sums of money had been contributed to the Conservative funds in various elections, and also that money had been subscribed on behalf of the Company to a cash testimonial presented to Sir John himself, and for stock in the *Mail* newspaper. The transaction was vigorously denounced by the Reform and Independent press as a specimen of brazen corruption.

GRIP, APRIL 7th, 1877.

WHAT INVESTIGATION REVEALED.

THE TOOLEY STREET TAILORS

Mr. Goldwin Smith's deliverances on the subject of Canada's destiny had an air of authority about them, suggestive of the idea that he was the accepted representative of the people. The notorious fact was that very few acknowledged sympathy with his views.

GRIP, APRIL 21st, 1877.

THE TAILORS OF TOOLEY STREET.

"WE, THE PEOPLE OF CANADA."

HOME FROM EPHESUS

At the close of the Session at Ottawa, Sir John Macdonald was received in Toronto by a party demonstration, embracing torch-lights and all the usual accompanyments of such occasions. As the Northern Railway revelations were at the moment occupying public attention, the procession was pictured as it should have been rather than as it was. Mr. John Beverley Robinson, M.P. for West Toronto, had shortly before this distinguished himself in a personal encounter with the proprietor of the Toronto *Telegram*. Sir John had, in a speech before the Session, declared that he and Robinson intended to "fight the beasts at Ephesus."

GRIP, MAY 5th, 1877.

"HOME FROM EPHESUS."

(THE TORCHLIGHT-RECEPTION, AS SEEN FROM A GRIT STANDPOINT.)

THE DANGERS OF DISSOLUTION

The Conservative reaction having now unquestionably set in, the *Mail* boldly challenged the Government to dissolve the House and appeal to the country.

GRIP, MAY 19th, 1877.

THE DANGER OF DISSOLUTION.

BILLED FOR THE SEASON

An active campaign was being conducted by the Conservative leaders, in anticipation of the general election. At political picnics in various parts of the country, Sir John Macdonald, Sir Charles Tupper and other leaders expatiated on the National Policy, and held up the "fly on the wheel" policy of the Government to scorn. Meantime, Mr. Patrick Boyle, of the *Irish Canadian*, continued to inveigh against "Scotch Supremacy."

GRIP, JUNE 9th, 1877.

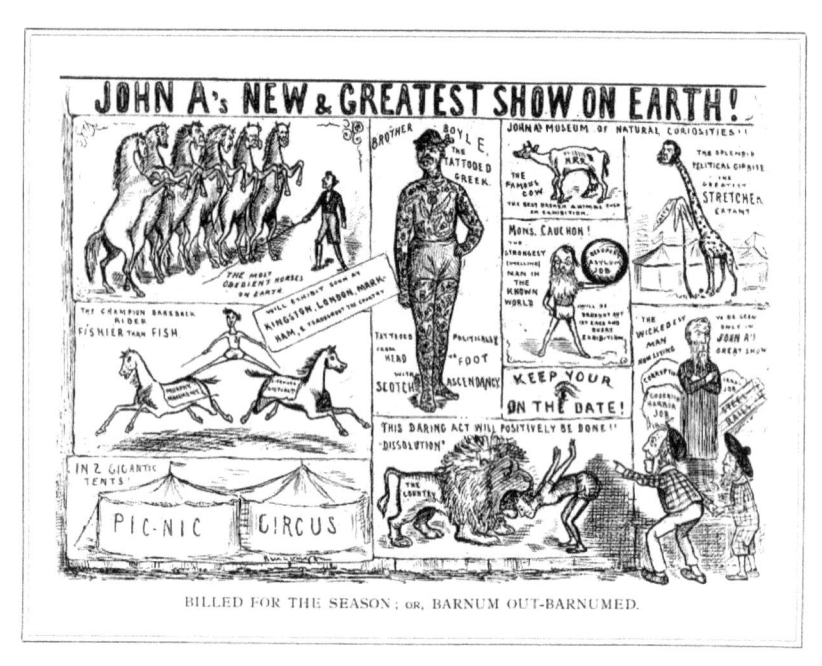

BILLED FOR THE SEASON; OR, BARNUM OUT-BARNUMED.

CATCHING THE ST. CATHARINES ROBBER

The election of Mr. C. J. Rykert as representative of Lincoln was contested by Mr. Norris, the defeated candidate. Before the decision was reached, certain documents material to the case disappeared from the Scrutiny Court. The Conservative Association offered a reward for the recovery of these papers, but as they were known to be in favor of the Grit candidate this action was regarded with suspicion. The cartoon contains an allusion to the well-known episode in Sir John's career—his fervent wish that he could catch Riel, whom it was afterwards found he had secretly sent out of the country.

GRIP, JUNE 28th, 1877.

"CATCHING THE ST. CATHARINES ROBBER."
(SHOWING HOW HISTORY RIEL-LY REPEATS ITSELF.)

THE BILL BOARD RE-DECORATED

Not to be outdone by the Tory Circus, the Grit Party managers organized for a political campaign, and held picnics in various districts at which the policy of the Government was defended, and the "hypocrisy" and "senselessness" of the N. P. cry were eloquently exposed.

GRIP, JULY 7th, 1877.

THE BILL BOARD RE-DECORATED.

WHAT THE CHIEFTAIN HEARD

Sir John professed to hear a universal demand for the reinstatement of himself and colleagues in office. It was not doubted that some sound had reached his ears, but GRIP'S view was that this sound was but the echo of his own anxious voice. In this GRIP was mistaken, however.

GRIP, JULY 14th, 1877.

WHAT THE CHIEFTAIN HEARD.

"WHEN I WAS IN THE EASTERN TOWNSHIPS, I HEARD THE CRY ECHOING FROM ROCK TO ROCK, ACROSS THE BOSOMS OF THOSE BEAUTIFUL LAKES, AND OVER THE EMERALD FIELD,—'COME TO OUR RESCUE, JOHN A., OR WE ARE LOST.'"

SIR JOHN'S SPEECH AT MONTREAL. SEE THE MAIL, JULY 9TH.

LET US HAVE PEACE

The *Globe* exerted all its influence to allay the bad feeling which had been manifested in connection with the Montreal riots between Orangemen and

Catholics, and which existed in many other parts of the country. It was strongly opposed, however, to the policy of prohibiting party processions by law, as this only tended to intensify the evil.

GRIP, AUGUST 4th, 1877.

LET US HAVE PEACE;

OR, THE BEST WAY TO END THE "PROCESSION" DIFFICULTY.

FRUITLESS OPPOSITION

The Mackenzie Government was assailed from time to time with charges of wrong doing, but the facts were in every case found to favor the Ministry.

One after another the "scandals" were dissipated, and the Opposition felt discouraged accordingly.

GRIP, AUGUST 25th, 1877.

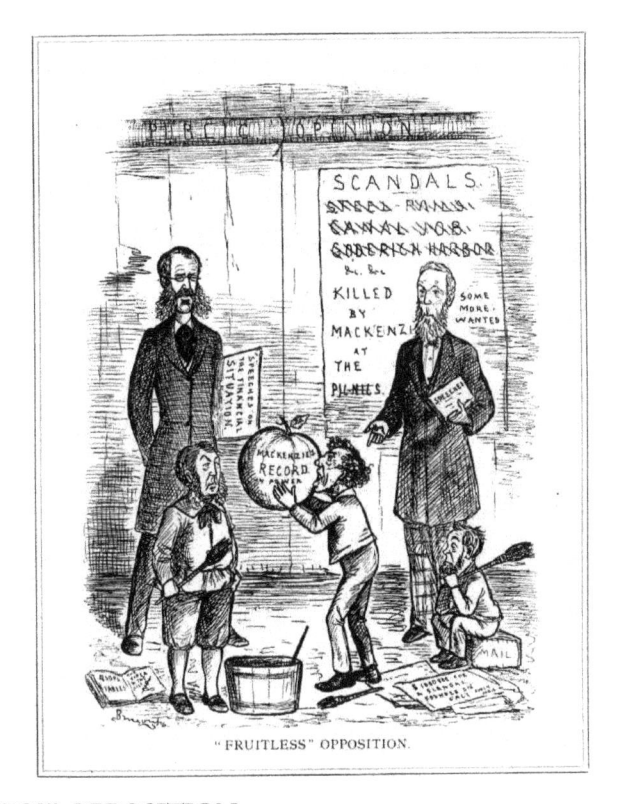

"FRUITLESS" OPPOSITION.

TEACHING THE POLLY-TICIANS WHAT TO SAY

The Pacific Scandal was by this date so far "Ancient History" that the facts of the case had undergone a complete metamorphosis as given out by the Tory orators. It was now the fashionable thing in that party to repeat the watchword given in the cartoon.

GRIP, SEPTEMBER 8th, 1877.

TEACHING THE POLLY-TICIANS WHAT TO SAY.

THE POLITICAL JONAH

Hon. Jos. Cauchon was appointed to the Lieutenant-Governorship of Manitoba, and thus what was generally regarded as the scandal of his connection with the Ministry was ended. That the appointment was made for the purpose of getting rid of him in the interests of the Government could not be questioned. M. Cauchon died a few years later while still filling the post of Lieutenant-Governor.

GRIP, SEPTEMBER 22nd, 1877.

THE POLITICAL JONAH; OR, SAVING THE SHIP.

THE NEEBING ROOKERY

For want of better ammunition for an attack upon the Dominion Government, the Opposition attempted to make out a scandal of the purchase by the authorities of a building known as the Neebing Hotel, at a point on the Lake Superior Section of the C. P. R., then in course of construction. It was alleged that the building was a tumble-down structure, for which an exorbitant price had been paid to the owner on the score of political partisanship. The triviality of the matter as the basis of a great Parliamentary fuss excited general amusement, especially as it proved that there was little if any ground for the charge made.

GRIP, SEPTEMBER 29th, 1877.

THE NEEBING ROOKERY.

A GREAT BOON TO THE OPPOSITION CROWS.

HON. WM. McPHARAOH'S DREAM

Hon. William Macdougall was thought to have made a mistake in associating himself with the Conservative Party if, as was generally alleged, the object he had in view was the great goal of most political aspirants—office. The Conservatives were now in the cold shades of Opposition, and to all appearance destined to remain there for a long time.

GRIP, OCTOBER 6th, 1877.

HON. WILLIAM McPHARAOH'S DREAM

OF THE FAT AND THE LEAN KINE.

HIS BEST FRIEND DESERTING HIM

The main hope of the Opposition in view of the general election was in the capital that was being made out of the depression of trade. A slight improvement was noticeable in the business outlook at the date of this cartoon.

GRIP, OCTOBER 20th, 1877.

HIS BEST FRIEND DESERTING HIM.

WHY THE REFORM PULLET DON'T HATCH HER EGGS

Having assumed the responsibilities of a Cabinet office, Mr. Blake allowed his advanced ideas to remain in abeyance. This silence on his part was attributed to the influence of Mr. Brown and the *Globe*, whose opposition to the projects advocated by Mr. Blake has already been alluded to.

GRIP, OCTOBER 27th, 1877.

WHY THE REFORM PULLET DON'T HATCH HER EGGS.

M—K—NZ—E.—"SHE'S AYE CLUCKING, BUT SHE ISNA ALLOOED TO SIT, YE SEE."

THE INNOXIOUS VIPER

Mr. Blake was the subject of a number of scurrilous articles in the *Mail*, and of several scandalous speeches by Conservative leaders. The charges, in so far as they concerned his private character, affected public opinion only against those who uttered them. In a speech at Teeswater, Mr. Blake replied in dignified and scathing terms to these criticisms.

GRIP, NOVEMBER 10th, 1877.

THE INNOXIOUS VIPER.

"AND HE SHOOK OFF THE BEAST INTO THE FIRE, AND FELT NO HARM."

THE POLITICAL PURITAN.

The Reform leaders still continued to assert it as one of the objects of the Reform Party to "elevate the standard of political morality," notwithstanding the damaging testimony of bribery, etc., which had been made public in connection with trials of petitions against various Members elect on that side of the House.

GRIP, NOVEMBER 17th, 1877.

THE POLITICAL PURITAN.

SCARING THE MARITIME HORSE

The free trade sentiment in the Maritime Provinces was known to be strong, and it was thought that the advocacy of the National Policy would endanger the seats of the Conservatives in that section of the country. Sir Charles Tupper was the leading representative of his party from the Lower Provinces, and was one of the most efficient supporters of the Protection idea. The event proved, however, that Sir Charles understood the temper of the people down by the sea better than the theorists, as the N. P. was handsomely sustained in that part of the country.

GRIP, NOVEMBER 24th, 1877.

SCARING THE MARITIME HORSE.

SETTLING THE ACCOUNT

The arbitrators appointed to decide the dispute between Canada and the United States in reference to the Fisheries had awarded the sum of $5,500,000 to the Dominion as compensation for damages sustained at the hands of American fishermen. To this award Mr. Kellogg, the American representative, had dissented, and had afterwards sought to invalidate the award on the ground that the decision had not been unanimous. The United States had not at that time—and have not yet—paid to England the large balance remaining from the Geneva award, promptly paid by the latter Power in connection with the "Alabama" claims.

GRIP, DECEMBER 1st, 1877.

SETTLING THE ACCOUNT.

JONATHAN.—"CRAWL OUT OF THAT LOOP-HOLE?"

HUNKERSLIDE.—"NEVER! KELLOGG, NEVER! I'LL PAY 'EM THE AWARD NOBLY—*WITH THEIR OWN MONEY!*"

ANXIOUS JOHNNY

The Conservative press had commented feelingly upon the fact that Mr. Blake was in poor health, and his retirement from official duties was kindly advised. The motive of this neighborly interest was open to question, in view of the recent attacks upon the gentleman concerned, and his influence as an opponent of the Conservative Party.

GRIP, DECEMBER 8th, 1878.

ANXIOUS JOHNNY,

WAITING FOR A CERTAIN PARTY TO "RETIRE."

SITTING ON THE POOR MAN

An agitation for the abolition of the system of exemption from taxation had been started in the newspapers. The injustice of exempting various officials who enjoyed good salaries, and imposing a corresponding heavy burden upon those less able to bear it, was earnestly denounced, and the Ontario Government were called upon to introduce a measure to cure the evil. No action has, however, been taken up to the present time.

GRIP, JANUARY 19th, 1878.

SITTING ON THE POOR MAN; OR, THE INJUSTICE OF EXEMPTION.

THE MYSTERIOUS HANDWRITING ON THE WALL

The confident prophesies of the Conservatives that the Government would certainly be defeated upon an appeal to the country were regarded as mere vaporings of those over anxious to return to the good things of office.

GRIP, FEBRUARY 23rd, 1878.

THE MYSTERIOUS HANDWRITING ON THE WALL.

THE RETIRING MINISTER

Mr. Blake retired from the Ministry on account of the unsatisfactory condition of his health. The allusions in this cartoon will be understood from the comments upon preceding pictures dealing with Mr. Blake.

GRIP, MARCH 2nd, 1878.

THE RETIRING MINISTER.

OUR FINANCIAL POE-SITION

Mr. (now Sir) Richard Cartwright, Finance Minister, announced a deficit in his budget speech. This furnished occasion for a vigorous attack upon the Government, and was regarded by the Opposition as emphasizing the necessity for a change of fiscal policy.

GRIP, MARCH 16th, 1878.

OUR FINANCIAL POE-SITION.

Hon. Richard John.—
"And my soul from out that shadow,
That lies floating on the floor,
Shall be lifted never more!"
Quoth the Raven, "Never more!"

REACTION INTELLIGENCE

The Conservative press allowed nothing which could be construed as evidence of a reaction to pass without judicious comment. Amid the unquestionable signs of a change of public feeling there were occasional occurrences which furnished consolation to the Reform Party—such as the defeat of the Conservative Government in Quebec. The persons represented in the cartoon, besides Sir John Macdonald, are Hon. Charles Tupper, Mr. Mackenzie Bowell, Hon. H. Langevin, Hon. Peter Mitchell, Mr. Palmer (a Maritime Province representative) and Mr. Bunster, of British Columbia. The latter gentleman was well-known as an anti-Chinese agitator. Mr. (now Senator) Plumb, to whom reference is made, was a Member of the Opposition somewhat noted for long addresses in Parliament.

GRIP, MARCH 23rd, 1878.

REACTION INTELLIGENCE.

THE CHIEFTAIN, HAVING WITHDRAWN FOR REFRESHMENT, LEARNS HOW THE CONSERVATIVE REACTION IS GETTING ON.

WILL HE GET IT?

The action of Lieutenant-Governor Letellier of Quebec (an appointee of the Liberal Government), in dismissing the Conservative Government of Mr. DeBoucherville, was alleged to be a Party move to put the Liberals in possession of the Provincial treasury. The Lieutenant-Governor's proceeding was roundly denounced as unconstitutional, and he was subsequently dismissed by Sir John Macdonald's Government on account of it.

GRIP, APRIL 27th, 1878.

WILL HE GET IT?

MAY-DAY IN QUEBEC

On the first of May the election made necessary by the dismissal of the DeBoucherville Government was held in the Province of Quebec, and resulted in a victory for the Liberal Party under the leadership of Hon. H. G. Joly.

GRIP, MAY 4th, 1878.

MAY-DAY IN QUEBEC.

GRAND JOLY-FICATION.

PARLIAMENTARY LANGUAGE PROHIBITED

In the House of Commons Sir John Macdonald and Hon. Charles Tupper had used very violent language in reference to Mr. Donald A. Smith in the course of a debate in which that gentleman's name came up.

GRIP, MAY 18th, 1878.

PARLIAMENTARY LANGUAGE PROHIBITED.

ON THEIR TRIAL

The political campaign was now at its height, the general election being fixed for September. The Government were charged with many sins of commission, and with one overwhelming sin of omission in the matter of tariff reform. This bill of indictment was pressed with unusual vigor, and the result, as will be subsequently seen, was a verdict for the Opposition.

GRIP, JUNE 1st, 1878.

ON THEIR TRIAL.

"GENERAL DISTRESS."

Hon. Dr. Tupper's suggestion for a cartoon representing the Finance Minister as General Distress giving the people the word of command "Starve!" was of course adopted by GRIP'S obliged artist. Certain liberties were, however, taken in interpreting the word "people" which may not exactly have met the honorable gentleman's idea. It was nevertheless true that the class of our population which at the moment exhibited most signs of starvation was the professional politicians of the Opposition.

GRIP, JUNE 8th, 1878.

GENERAL DISTRESS.

"WERE I BENGOUGH, I WOULD REPRESENT MR. CARTWRIGHT AS *GENERAL DISTRESS*, GIVING THE PEOPLE THE WORD OF COMMAND—'STARVE!'"

DR. TUPPER, AS QUOTED BY HON. D. MILLS IN A RECENT SPEECH.

THE PEERLESS PEER

Lord Dufferin had attained to a popularity unequalled by any of our Governors-General since the days of Lord Elgin, and his departure from Canada called forth expressions of sincere regret from all classes. It was difficult to convince the Canadian people that the Home authorities would find it possible to secure a successor in all respects equal to Dufferin.

GRIP, JUNE 22nd, 1878.

THE PEERLESS PEER;
OR, JOHN BULL DIOGENES LOOKING FOR ANOTHER DUFFERIN.

ANCIENT TROY TACTICS

This was still another repetition of the opinion that the Tory Party, in adopting the National Policy, had in view the one grand object of "getting in" to office. The allusion is of course to the familiar classic story of the method adopted by the Greeks to gain admission to Troy.

GRIP, JULY 6th, 1878.

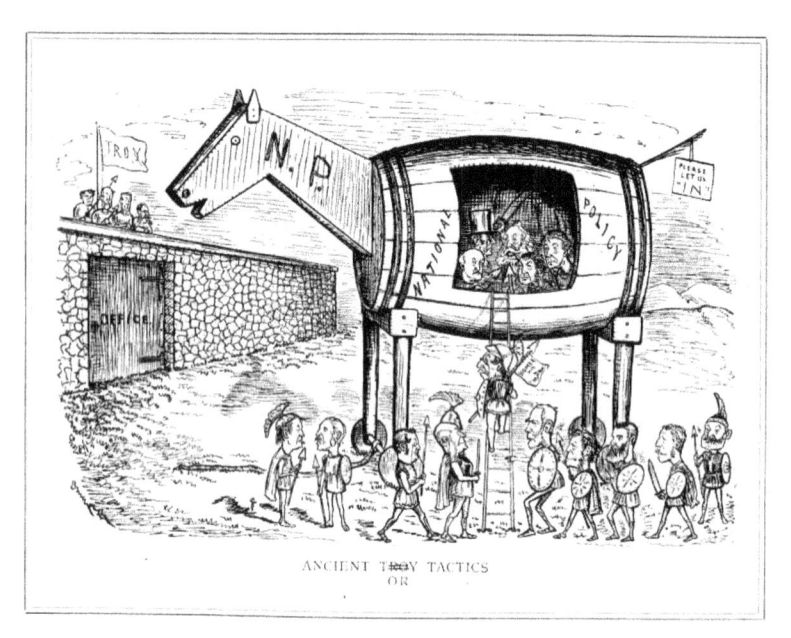

ANCIENT ~~TROY~~ TORY TACTICS.

THE TRULY LOYAL BOY ALARMING THE MASTER

A great outcry was made by the *Globe* on the alleged anti-British tendency of the National Policy as announced by the Conservative leaders during the campaign. To the alarming statement that it would inevitably weaken British connection, the leading organ of the Opposition responded—"so much the worse for British connection."

GRIP, JULY 27th, 1878.

THE TRULY LOYAL BOY ALARMING THE MASTER.

THE POLITICAL CONJURER

An amusing feature of the campaign was the contradictory nature of the Protectionist utterances. In Ontario Sir John Macdonald declared that if returned to power, he would vigorously protect native industries by shutting out foreign imports. This deliverance created alarm in the Lower Provinces, and in reply to an anxious enquiry from Senator Boyd, of St. John, N. B., upon the subject, the astute leader promptly declared that he had no intention of doing more than readjusting the duties. Mr. W. H. Frazer, who figures in this and some subsequent cartoons, was at the time an active official of the Ontario Manufacturers' Association, and an ardent Protectionist.

GRIP, AUGUST 3rd, 1878.

THE GREAT POLITICAL CONJURER.

"ALL SORTS OF WINE POURED OUT OF ONE AND THE SAME BOTTLE."

ALL AT SEA

Another allusion to the ludicrous contradictions and inconsistencies of the principal advocates of the National Policy in their public speeches, when, in response to the popular demand, they undertook to "come down to particulars" as to what that Policy was to be.

GRIP, AUGUST 17th, 1878.

"ALL AT SEA!"

CAPTAIN JOHN A.—"FOR GRACIOUS' SAKE, LADS, GET INTO SOME SHAPE! IF THAT SQUALL STRIKES US IN THIS CONDITION WE'LL NEVER GET IN!!"

THE NATIONAL POLICY MINSTRELS

The point as to how a revenue was to be obtained under an exclusive tariff without a resort to direct taxation was of course raised by the opponents of the Protective theory, and no satisfactory answer had been given to the "conundrum" up to the date of this cartoon.

GRIP, AUGUST 31st, 1878.

THE NATIONAL POLICY MINSTRELS.

BRUDDER TAMBO'S ASTOUNDING FINANCIAL CONUNDRUM.

WILL HE CAPTURE IT?

A promise of a seat in the prospective Tory Cabinet was made to Mr. John O'Donohue on condition that he would manage the "Catholic vote" in the Conservative interest in the forthcoming election. This reward Mr. O'Donohue did his best to win, but by the intervention of the Orange leaders, the "bargain" as made was not allowed to take effect. Mr. O'Donohue never got the portfolio, but had to content himself with a Senatorship instead.

GRIP, SEPTEMBER 7th, 1878.

WILL HE "CAPTURE" IT?

RENEWING THE LEASE

This bold prophecy was made on the assumption that the people of Canada clearly saw through the game of the newly-made Protectionists, and that the circumstances under which Sir John and his colleagues had demitted office in 1873 would preclude the possibility of their success on this occasion.

GRIP, SEPTEMBER 14th, 1878.

RENEWING THE LEASE.

MISS CANADA (TO JOHN A.)—"YOU WANT THE FARM AGAIN! YOU LEFT IT IN A SHOCKING CONDITION FIVE YEARS AGO, AND THE PRESENT TENANT HAS ALMOST RESTORED IT BY HIS INDUSTRY. YOUR 'PLAN' LOOKS BOGUS. I WILL RENEW MACKENZIE'S LEASE."

O, OUR PROPHETIC SOUL!

The general election which came off on the 17th resulted in a sweeping victory for Sir John and the National Policy, and Mr. GRIP'S artist humbly took his place amongst the false prophets.

O, OUR PROPHETIC SOUL!

(See last week's Cartoon.)

JOHN A.—"I DON'T KNOW, BUT IT SEEMS TO ME THIS PICTURE OF YOURS, MY PROPHETIC FRIEND, NEEDS A LITTLE 'RE-ADJUSTMENT,' DON'T IT, HEY?"

RIDING INTO POWER

In anticipation of the difficulty the new Ministry would meet in reconciling the various conflicting trade interests in the promised tariff changes, the N. P. was referred to as a White Elephant—a beast proverbially awkward to have on hand. That the Policy had proved a particularly "happy thought" on the part of the Conservative leader was now manifest, for it is doubtful if anything excepting this adroit appeal to the people's pockets could possibly have restored the Conservatives to power at this time.

GRIP, SEPTEMBER 28th, 1878.

RIDING INTO POWER.

CAREFUL HANDLING REQUIRED

Amongst the most able—and one of the few sincere—advocates of the National Policy, was Mr. R. W. Phipps, a well-known journalist and pamphleteer of Toronto. Sir John had during the campaign publicly accorded high praise to this gentleman for his writings in support of Protection; and indeed so great was the indebtedness expressed that Mr. Phipps came to believe that he would certainly be offered the portfolio of Finance in the New Government. Mr. Phipps, on the other hand, made no secret of his own conviction that neither Sir John nor any of his colleagues really understood the principles of political economy.

GRIP, OCTOBER 12th, 1878.

CAREFUL HANDLING REQUIRED!

JOHN A.'S NEW MARIONETTES

The names of the Members of the new Cabinet were duly announced as given in the cartoon. Mr. Phipps was disappointed in the matter of a portfolio, and still further in the absence from the list of Ministers of the name of any person known to be a sincere Protectionist. It was alleged that Hon. William Macdougall had also entertained hopes of a seat in the Cabinet. The Manufacturers' Association began to exhibit great activity in view of the forthcoming Tariff changes.

GRIP, OCTOBER 26th, 1878.

JOHN A.'S NEW MARIONETTES.

THE BEST OF FRIENDS MUST PART

To the hard times Sir John and his Party were primarily indebted for their present good fortune, but (contrary to the hopes of the innocents who had implicitly accepted the anti-election promises of the N. P. advocates) prosperity did not immediately return. The persistency with which the depression continued to "hang on" was a source of much annoyance to the Government, as it was the constant theme of ridicule in the Reform press.

GRIP, NOVEMBER 2nd, 1878.

"THE BEST OF FRIENDS MUST PART!"

JOHN A.—"WELL, GOOD-BY, OLD FELLOW; THANKS VERY MUCH FOR YOUR HELP DURING THE CAMPAIGN; BUT DON'T LET ME DETAIN YOU NOW. GOOD-BY, *AU REVOIR*, ADIEU, FAREWELL, TRA-LA-LA, TA-TA."

HARD TIMES.—"CERTINGLY; BUT I AIN'T GONE YET, ME HEARTY!"

RICHARD'S HIMSELF AGAIN

Sir Richard Cartwright, who had been defeated in the general election, was now returned for the constituency of Centre Huron. As the keenest financial critic in the ranks of the Reform Opposition, his presence in the House was considered a Party necessity in view of the prospective introduction of the new fiscal regulations.

GRIP, NOVEMBER 9th, 1878.

RICHARD'S HIMSELF AGAIN!

HURRYING UP THE ELEPHANT

Curiosity was on tiptoe throughout the country during the interim between the election and the introduction of the National Policy. The Reform press aggravated the popular impatience by constant—and not very reasonable—protests against the delay. Indeed, some of the precipitous journalists went so far as to assert that the Government had no intention of inaugurating a new fiscal policy at all.

GRIP, NOVEMBER 30th, 1878.

HURRYING UP THE ELEPHANT!

CLAMORING FOR THE FANCY DOLL

This cartoon is perhaps so obvious as to need no comment. The general feeling in the Reform Party in favor of the retirement of Mr. Mackenzie from the leadership, in favor of Mr. Blake, was not warmly shared by the *Globe*. When ultimately the change was effected a degree of dissatisfaction was expressed in some quarters where the impression obtained that Mr. Mackenzie had not been generously treated in the matter.

GRIP, DECEMBER 7th, 1878.

CLAMORING FOR THE FANCY DOLL.